MARRIAGE TAKES MORE THAN LOVE

JACK and CAROLE MAYHALL

NAVPRESS
A MINISTRY OF THE NAVIGATORS
P.O. Box 6000, Colorado Springs, Colorado 80934

The Navigators is an international, evangelical Christian organization. Jesus Christ gave His followers the Great Commission to go and make disciples (Matthew 28:19). The aim of The Navigators is to help fulfill that commission by multiplying laborers for Christ in every nation.

NavPress is the publishing ministry of The Navigators. NavPress publications are tools to help Christians grow. Although publications alone cannot make disciples or change lives, they can help believers learn biblical discipleship, and apply what they learn to their lives and ministries.

Seventh printing, 1981

Unless otherwise identified, Scripture quotations are from the *New American Standard Bible*, © 1960, 1962, 1963, 1968, 1971, 1972, 1973, 1975 by The Lockman Foundation. Other versions used are the *King James Version* (KJV); the *Amplified New Testament* (AMP), © 1954, 1958, by The Lockman Foundation; *The Living Bible* (LB), © 1971 by Tyndale House Publishers, Wheaton, Illinois; and *The New Testament in Modern English, Revised Edition* by J.B. Phillips (PH), © 1958, 1960, 1972 by J.B. Phillips, published by The Macmillan Company, New York and Collins Publishers, London.

Printed in the United States of America

CONTENTS

to Joye and Fred
rich in wisdom
rich in love

"I thank my God
upon every remembrance of you"

AUTHORS

JACK and Carole Mayhall work with The Navigators, an international, interdenominational Christian organization committed to helping carry out Christ's Great Commission in this generation. Jack serves as Executive Vice-president and Divisional Director for the United States, while Carole is active with Navigator wives in Colorado Springs, Colorado, and has a ministry with women nationwide.

Jack was raised in Peoria, Illinois, and graduated from Wheaton College (Illinois) and Dallas Theological Seminary. He was ordained in 1954 and served as Assistant Pastor and Youth Director at the First Presbyterian Church in Aurora, Illinois and at Central Bible Church in Portland, Oregon.

Carole graduated from high school in a small town in southern Michigan, from Wheaton College with a degree in Christian education, and was the education director at a Columbus, Ohio church for a year before she married Jack in 1949.

The Mayhalls joined the Navigator staff in 1956 and have ministered in a variety of responsibilities in Colorado, California, and Illinois. They have one daughter, Lynn, who is married to Tim Westburg.

In addition to his management responsibilities, Jack is a sought-after speaker at conferences and seminars. Carole also frequently speaks at conferences and seminars, and at Women's Clubs around the country. She has written *From the Heart of a Woman* (NavPress, 1976), and *Lord, Teach Me Wisdom* (NavPress, 1979).

This book is based on a seminar on marriage that Jack and Carole have presented throughout the United States and in England and Norway as well. It has been given to a wide spectrum of groups, including communities, churches, and various conferences.

FOREWORD

A GOOD marriage, most people say, has no serious problems, while a poor marriage is one in which there are many problems. Not so, we believe. Problems go along with people—in and out of marriage. If you don't have problems, you're probably paralyzed.

The difference between smooth sailing and shipwreck in marriage lies in what you as a couple are doing about the rough weather. All marriages have strengths and weaknesses. All marriages are either dynamic or they are deteriorating. The husband-wife combo must either progress or perish.

Volumes have been written on why marriages fail, but only a trickle of helpful advice on the care and cultivation of good relationships has reached the bookshelves. Many couples are frustrated and despairing because they do not know how to reverse the downward trend in their lives together.

Jack and Carole Mayhall have written *Marriage Takes More Than Love* from rich personal experience to help revitalize marriages, fresh or stale. Their key is "working at it." But how? By pointing out individual responsibility, by reinforcng these concepts with scriptural principles, and by illustrating their workability from their own lives.

Overseas missionaries report that the distinctively Christian home is what makes the greatest impact on a pagan culture. Western culture, once Christian, thirsts deeply for the return of this purifying core of home life. This book points toward that goal.

HOWARD AND JEANNE HENDRICKS

PREFACE

SPEAKING of kissing! We weren't, of course, but let's. When our daughter was five, she had a whole repertoire of kisses. She had the eyelash-against-cheek "butterfly," the rub-noses "Eskimo," the starting-at-one-side-around-face-to-other-side "sliding" kiss, and the old-fashioned "smack."

Such diversity also exists today in describing marriages, ranging from happy to good to mediocre to awful to hopeless. But only 3% claim the "happy" label. A few more hope for "good," but most openly admit it is a pretty ghastly marriage-go-round they're riding.

Today the marriage picture looks so dark that light and shadow have little contrast on the screen. We don't wonder why so many marriages fall apart; rather, we are amazed that any hang together.

Forces seem to be striking us over which we have no control. And the more prophets of doom shriek around us, the more obsessed we become with our own failures and inadequacies.

But GOD . . . !

It is a fact that the divorce rate in the United States of America is rapidly approaching the 50% mark. We see around us a degenerating society lapping up the salt water of self-destruction, trying to satisfy an unquenchable thirst for something always just beyond reach. We hear story after story of broken relationships, unhappy homes, and miserable marriages.

But GOD . . . !

It takes three persons to make a satisfying marriage. A husband, a wife, and God. Marriage can be a beautiful, deeply satisfying, fulfilling relationship But only *because* God is in it.

God created, designed, and planned marriage He then initiated a plan to insure that it would work That plan is given in the Bible and in the Book of Ephesians is called the "walk" of the Christian. Biblically, this "walk" is how a Christian is to live day by day, progressing one obedient step at a time and listening carefully to God's voice as He speaks through His Word. Apart from that walk—obeying God in our lives—a lasting, loving relationship is incredibly difficult to achieve.

But with God's leading and help, as two people progress and grow in love, a happy marriage is a cinch . . . well, not quite a cinch. It does take two essential ingredients forever and always.

One ingredient is prayer, for without God's power this walk in love is impossible.

The other is a determination on the part of both to work at this relationship. Marriage cannot be put on autopilot.

Committed to these ingredients, any couple can build a relationship that reflects Christ's love for His Church.

This is a "his and her" book. Not only do we hope that you will read it *together* as an engaged or married couple, but it is presented from two points of view. A "his and her" view. You will find the outlooks different. But we trust you will find one essential message.

It is our prayer that some of the things God has taught us in the last 30 years of knowing one another will help you fall more deeply in love—with each other and with the God who created us all.

JACK AND CAROLE MAYHALL
COLORADO SPRINGS, COLORADO, 1978

SECTION I

The Basis for a Successful Marriage

1

CHOOSING A FOUNDATION
by Jack

I GLANCED up from the tennis court to where Carole was watching and grinned. We exchanged a wink and a glance that said, *Hi. I'm glad you're here. Thanks for being you.*

As I resumed play, I thought of the numerous times we have shared such moments. Thirty years ago it was a football field instead of a tennis court. Aware of Carole yelling encouragement from the stands of our small college, I would look up and wave. Through the years the scene has changed from basketball courts to handball courts to golf courses and currently to tennis courts.

These have been moments of sharing which have soldered intimacy to the framework of our lives. Carole and I have deliberately *chosen* to share these moments together.

All of marriage is a choice. One small choice follows on the heels of another till the trail becomes clear and worn. The right choices make for intimacy and closeness—a oneness in marriage that equals no other relationship on the human level. Wrong choices start a couple on the road to disenchantment, loneliness, emotional and perhaps physical separation.

13

One such choice is not a conscious one for most of us. Yet it is even more important than the choice of a partner for life. It is deciding the foundation on which the marriage will rest.

I am not sure that Carole and I ever gave conscious thought to this foundation. We met, fell in love, went together in college for three-and-a-half years, got engaged, unengaged, engaged again (we had a rather stormy time of it and broke our engagement three times), and *finally* walked down the aisle in a wood-frame church in a small Michigan town. I was a bit late for the wedding, the best man lost the wedding ring (his wife found it a few minutes after the ceremony), but nothing could rob us of that moment we had been anticipating for so long.

But we had not thought through on goals and objectives, on what we really wanted our marriage and our lives to be based.

However, we had a number of things going for us. Love was exemplified in both our home backgrounds. We observed a great deal in the lives of our parents without being actively aware of what deep truths we were learning. As children, both of us had invited Jesus Christ to come into our lives, to be our Lord and Saviour, and we had begun to experience Christ leading us day by day.

Each of us had prayed for some time, and we knew our parents had long prayed as well concerning God's choice of a life-partner. When we said, "I do," we were confident that God had answered those prayers.

Finally, we knew the truth of the psalmist's statement, "Unless the Lord builds the house, they labor in vain who build it" (Psalm 127:1). God builds that "house" from scratch.

MARRIAGE IS GOD'S IDEA

The great foundation stone of marriage was dug and firmly laid in place at the creation of the world. Man may think that marriage was his idea, but man is wrong.

Genesis is the book of beginnings, and records the story of the creation in the first chapter. When God finished each day's work, He surveyed the world and declared, "It is good!" But on the sixth day, when man and woman were created, the Lord looked out over His vast creation and said, "It is *very* good!" (Genesis 1:31)

That says something to me. God wasn't just a *little* pleased over the job He had done in creating man and woman. He was *enormously* satisfied. When God leads two people together, puts a love in their hearts for each other, and joins them in the bond of marriage, that is a unique creation. The touch of God's hand is on that new relationship.

In the second chapter of the Book of Genesis, God gives us some insights into the *details* of what happened on that momentous sixth day. In a beautiful account, He explains how Adam and Eve got together.

Use your imagination and picture yourself in the Garden of Eden. I don't know what the Garden of Eden would be for you (our pictures will probably be different), but for me it would probably have at least two 18-hole golf courses (Robert Trent Jones designed), beautifully laid out.

Adam was in a paradise that was everything his heart could desire in terms of beauty and satisfaction. He had it made. He even had the privilege of taking walks with God. Yes, the Lord Himself walked with Adam.

Yet as God looked into the heart of this man whom He had created, He saw something there that caused Him to ponder. Something was missing. So God said, "He's lonely. He is all alone. I will make for him a helper fit for him" (see Genesis 2:18).

A great search began. "Out of the ground the Lord God formed every beast of the field and every bird of the sky, and brought them to the man to see what he would call them; and whatever the man called a living creature, that was its name. But for Adam there was not found a helper suitable [or fit] for him" (2:19-20).

God and Adam looked everywhere, but they didn't find anything that would meet his need. "So the Lord God caused a deep sleep to fall upon the man, and he slept; then He took one of his ribs, and closed up the flesh at that place. And the Lord God fashioned into a woman the rib which He had taken from the man, and brought her to the man. And the man said, 'This is now bone of my bones, and flesh of my flesh; she shall be called Woman, because she was taken out of Man' " (2:21-23).

Can you put yourself into that situation? Here was Adam in these beautiful surroundings. He was still rubbing sleep from his eyes when all of a sudden, out of the trees, walked a gorgeous creature. He had never seen one like this before; he had never seen a *woman*. And he got excited about it.

He may have let out a long whistle and yelled out, "Wow! At last!" He was thoroughly impressed.

And that was the start of marriage, for the passage goes on, "For this cause a man shall leave his father and his mother, and shall cleave to his wife; and they shall become one flesh" (2:24). This command is repeated three other times in the Bible, that a man shall *leave,* and *cleave,* and the two shall become *one* flesh (Matthew 19:5; Mark 10:7-8; Ephesians 5:31).

Marriage is God's idea. It was His creative plan and He made it beautiful. It is man who has disfigured and marred it, but it need not be so.

MARRIAGE CAN BE SUCCESSFUL

Most of us want to be successful in our marriages. We don't get married determined to fail. A national survey once indicated that 80% of Americans over age 18 choose "a happy family life" as their number one goal. A happy family life was selected over the opportunity to develop as an individual, or a fulfilling career, or making money. Some 75% of the respondents also agreed with the statement, "The traditional family is important to American society and should be preserved."

We live in an age which provides an atmosphere that causes most married couples to have almost everything going against them for success. Yet the Apostle Paul's statement, "If God is for us, who is against us?" (Romans 8:31) is as true today as when it was written.

God is still in the business of creating marriages. He desires to be the foundation stone of each union. Most marriages are based on nothing; it is not surprising that many collapse.

But it is never too late with God. At any point, if we will turn over our lives and our marriages to Him, He will become the foundation, the builder, and the rebuilder, if that is necessary, of that home. Even the broken pieces of our lives can be mended and repaired if we let God be God in every area of our human relationships.

2

CHOOSING GOD AS LORD
by Carole

IT HAPPENED in the middle of one of the three times Jack and I had broken our engagement. I was miserable. Miserable because Jack's ring was no longer on my finger. But even more unhappy because I had lost the *feeling* of God's presence. With anxiety and tears I sought the Lord time after time, asking Him for His comfort and peace. My prayers seemed to ricochet off the light fixture, bounce off the desk, and lie in a miserable heap at my feet. I wasn't getting through.

I said, "Lord, what's the matter? I need You now more than ever before. Don't You hear me? Please tell me what is wrong."

And He got through to me.

Since becoming one of His children, I had assured God that if He wanted me to be single, I would be willing. And I meant it. However, that was *before* I fell in love with Jack. Subtly the picture had changed. I couldn't view life without Jack anymore. I felt that if God didn't give Jack to me, my life would be second-rate at best.

But God would have no rival in my life. He was teaching me a deep lesson through this experience of heartache. Finally, as I cried and prayed, He convinced me that His will was *perfect;* it was *best* for me. If marrying Jack was His *second* best, would I really want that for my life?

I struggled with that one for a while because it was hard for me to conceive that life with Jack *could* be second best. At last I surrendered my will to God and said, "Whatever is Your *first* best for me, Father, whatever will bring You the most glory *even if it means being single for the rest of my life,* that is what I want. Please help me want Your will in my life above everything else. Help me want more of You because I know that only You can truly satisfy."

In that moment, I felt as though the ceiling and roof rolled away and I had direct access to heaven itself! God's presence, His comfort, and His peace shoved my empty spiritual gauge to FULL.

A few months later, God led us together again —permanently this time, for which I have been forever grateful. A lasting lesson seared my heart that day which burned the knowledge on my mind that *no* human being, no matter how wonderful, can satisfy the longings of the human heart. Only God can do that. There really *is* a "God-shaped vacuum in every human heart which only God can fill."

God has blessed me with a loving and tender husband. Jack is all that I could ask for in a mate. God has also given us a daughter who is walking with Him and is now married to a wonderful man. They continually rejoice our hearts. But even with these and all the other blessings of life, an emptiness and futility would remain within—*except for God.*

I have seen too many wives try to force their husbands to meet their every need—a feat no human can do—and in the forcing have destroyed what could have been a beautiful relationship.

God meant a husband and a wife to be two whole, complete individuals. Complete in Him. When these two complete individuals, having their needs met by God Himself, come together in a marriage designed by Him, they equal more than two. They multiply to four or eight or a hundred. I don't mean children. I mean the impact of their lives and ministries. But if we marry as only a part of a person, and then depend on our mates for survival, we become parasites that feed on the other spouse, draining our own lives of joy and fulfillment.

It took me a while to learn this. Jack has always been a good "need-meeter." It wasn't till a change in jobs caused him to travel almost half the time that I finally learned a needed lesson.

At first, when Jack was away and couldn't meet my needs, I became dissatisfied and frustrated. Then God began to teach me a deep truth about Himself. He really meant it when He said that He could and would satisfy my every need. He began to be my Companion, my Comfort, and my Joy in a new way.

Only the puzzle pieces were not fitting together. One time when Jack was home, he said to me, "Sometimes I get the feeling that I'm not needed around here anymore!"

My heart sank. What a terrible impression to leave with the one I love most on this earth. I immediately made some "set apart" time to ask God about that one. And God made it clear to me. He put the jigsaw pieces together in my thinking.

Yes, God alone meets my needs. But when He gave Jack to me, He chose to meet those needs, many times, *through* my husband. At other times, He meets them through Lynn, my daughter, or relatives or friends. When He chooses to meet my need of companionship, comfort, tenderness, joy through my husband or others, He will do it in *no other way.* So I am totally dependent on Jack at that time. However, if Jack can't (or in a very few cases, won't) meet my needs, there is no cause for frustration or unhappiness. Because God *can and will* meet those needs! He is reaching out to meet the needs of our hearts.

A sign on a church bulletin board read, "God can mend a broken heart, if you will give Him all the pieces." God can also mend a broken marriage . . . if you will give Him all the pieces. He can take a shattered marriage and glue it together so perfectly that it will not even show the cracks. He will make it stronger than it was before it shattered. Or He can take a good marriage and make it more beautiful every day.

The secret lies in giving it *all* to Him. And before that can be done with a marriage, it has to be done by the individuals that form the marriage. Perhaps the greatest prayer a wife or husband can pray is, "Lord, save this marriage, *beginning with me!*" Or, "Change this marriage, *beginning with me!*"

James Jauncey, eminent Australian educator, says:

Many women have asked wistfully: "Why could it not always be like when we were first married?" Well, it can. The newness and the excitement die down, of course, and the emotional froth subsides somewhat. Couples tend to get used to anything in time. But a deep romantic love can continue as if the soul is being fed by some inner springs. If you have lost that love, the fountain hasn't dried up. You have ceased to tap it, that's all.

This is true not only of marriage, but of life itself. Everything about living can begin to pall unless we have hidden resources to replenish what is being depleted. All of life was intended to be a vibrant experience.[1]

We have to tap that resource. God is the source of love, of understanding, of acceptance. As we put our roots down deeply into Him, there flows into us a never-ending supply (see Isaiah 37:31; Jeremiah 17:7-8). Walter Trobisch, European pastor, teacher, and missionary to Africa, says that "love is a feeling to be learned"[2] and this is true. We have to *learn* to love—*really* love—and we learn it from God.

I've had women tell me that they have lost all feeling for their husbands; all respect, all love. They feel helpless and trapped and so they would be, without the power and strength of the Source. He alone can teach us to love deeply, in the way that we long to love the person to whom we are married.

But it has to begin with me. I cannot change my husband, but I can let the God of the universe change me. And in changing me into the kind of wife, the kind of person He wants me to be, my marriage will inevitably be altered.

I am not just half a couple. I am a complete child of God united with another complete child of God. And this is such a wondrous thing that nothing on earth comes close to it. With God as our unshakable foundation, our love will endure forever.

"So overflowing is His kindness towards us that He took away all our sins through the blood of His Son, by whom we are saved; and He has showered down upon us the richness of His grace—for how well He understands us and knows what is best for us at all times" (Ephesians 1:7-9, LB).

NOTES: 1. From *Magic in Marriage* by James H. Jauncey, page 9.
Copyright © 1966 by Zondervan Publishing House.
Used by permission.
2. Walter Trobisch, *Love Is a Feeling to Be Learned*
(Copyright © 1971 by Editions Trobisch, D-737 Baden
Baden, Germany. Published by InterVarsity Press,
Downers Grove, Illinois), page 9.

3

CHOOSING THE ARCHITECT
by Jack

THAT Saturday morning in March was one of those spectacular warm days we get in Colorado in late winter. It had been an unusually long, cold season, and as I glanced out the window toward Pike's Peak, the 14,000-foot mountain that overlooks the city, I thought, *What a perfect day for my first golf game this year!* By the time I had shaved and dressed, I was so psyched up for that golf game, I could think of little else than to be out there on the golf course.

Carole, still not being able to read my thoughts after 25 years of marriage, prepared a nice breakfast. Then, as we sat down to eat, she remarked, "Honey, it is such a beautiful day [I certainly agreed with that], wouldn't it be fun to go on a picnic and take a hike?"

I didn't say a word. But I thought, *Now that has got to be the dumbest idea she ever thought up.*

The day suddenly didn't look so good after all. I got moody, grumpy, and silent. And Carole didn't even know what had happened.

I didn't tell her what was going on in my mind; instead, I pouted inside for hours. I ruined the day. We didn't go on a picnic, and I didn't play golf.

Early in the afternoon, God finally got through to me and showed me what a DRA (in our household that stands for Dirty Rotten Attitude) I was having. And God called it by name—sin. He called it that because that is exactly what it was. I was being selfish, unkind, and mean.

Finally, I confessed it to God, asked Carole's forgiveness, and we managed to salvage a part of that day by spending some time together.

DEMONSTRATING LOVE

It is not always easy to demonstrate love, to be kind, to respond as Christ would. And the most difficult place to do this is at home.

The Apostle Paul, in his beautiful letter to the Ephesians, talks about three major subjects: the wealth (1:1—3:20), the walk (4:1—6:10), and the warfare (6:11-24) of a Christian. First, Paul tells us of the wealth that we possess simply by being children of God through Jesus Christ. Then he talks about how Christians are to live their daily lives. He concludes by telling us of the warfare against Satan in which we are constantly engaged. The key passage about the marriage relationship comes, not in the warfare section as some might think, but right in the center of the discussion on what it means *to walk* as a believer.

One of the goals God has for us—our walk in Christ —is for us to grow up in Him, to become mature people (4:13). The important ingredients for that maturity are the characteristics of kindness, understanding, and forgiveness; Paul states clearly, "Be kind to one another, tender-hearted, forgiving each other, just as God in Christ also has forgiven you" (4:32).

Our Christian life, then, is to be a walk of love, which

is learning to respond to each other in a continually loving way (5:2), and a walk of wisdom, which is growing in the understanding and discernment of Jesus Christ (5:15). Now if there are any two things that we need to make a successful marriage, it is love and wisdom; and these come only from God.

BEING FILLED WITH THE HOLY SPIRIT

The Apostle Paul continues and commands his readers—the Ephesians and us—to be "filled with the Spirit" (5:18). Without going into a theological treatise on this, being filled with the Spirit means that we let the Holy Spirit of God control how we act and what we say; we let Him have His way in our lives.

Sometimes that is extremely difficult. Being filled with the Spirit may not seem so hard when we are preparing for a Sunday School class, for a Bible study group, or a message. Most of us are unsure of ourselves in situations like these and fully aware that we cannot do them in our own strength. We have no choice but to pray that God will take over for us, and He does.

But when our guards are down, like in our own homes, it can be another story. Because life is so daily, many things come up in its course that make it difficult for us to *act* like Christians, especially toward those we love the most.

On that beautiful Saturday morning in March when I wanted to play golf, my guard was down and the enemy of my soul got off a shot which pierced my armor. I was anything but "filled with the Spirit."

I spoke in the opening session of a large conference in California shortly after moving to Colorado, and I felt totally inadequate for the situation. I prayed a great deal about it and had many others praying for me as well. I asked the Lord to speak through me, and the whole conference went beautifully. The Lord blessed it, using my message in the lives of many.

Then I got home.

We had moved into a new house three months before, and winter by now had set in. We had to install a new humidifier on the furnace. (In Colorado it is so dry that unless you put humidity in the air, the static electricity is so bad that every time you kiss your wife, the sparks literally fly.) When we returned home, the humidifier had leaked all over the floor into the furnace, which was now standing in a couple of inches of water.

That night, a snowstorm blew in from the north, our first since moving into that house. We have double doors that face north. The next morning we got up and found that we had almost enough snow in our hallway to make a snowman. Well, a few snowballs at least! Now a door just isn't supposed to do that.

Yes, there are times when it is very difficult to be filled with the Spirit.

BUILDING A MARRIAGE

All kinds of daily situations come up in our lives which affect our relationships with one another as husband and wife and cause us to cast ourselves on the Lord. On these, "the dailies of life," as Carole calls them, rest the balance of the scales. To respond as one who is filled with the Spirit weights the "happy marriage" side; to respond in our own flesh may put the balance on "miserable."

I really don't know anything about building houses. And I'd be a fool to try to build a house without a competent architect planning every board for me.

I don't know that much about building marriages

either—and I only intend to build *one.* I would be a greater fool not to let the Creator of marriage be my Architect. He wants to make a beautiful creation from each relationship given to Him. But He won't force His services on us. He waits to be asked. Right responses are only possible if we allow God to be in complete control. His Spirit alone can and will give us victory in areas where we are weak and defenseless.

A growing relationship with God and turning your marriage over to Him as Resident Architect and Builder will result in His helping you respond as one "filled with the Spirit" in the daily affairs of life.

SECTION II

Understanding One Another

4

CHOOSING TO UNDERSTAND
by Carole

JACK appeared in the doorway just as I breezed in the back door and set a bag of groceries on the kitchen table. He was wearing a blue shirt and a peculiar look which I could not read. He said, "Please come upstairs. I need to talk to you."

Now? How strange! I thought. Wondering, I followed him up the stairs, leaving the groceries to be unpacked later.

As we sat on the bed, Jack took both my hands in his. "Before I tell you something, I'd like to remind you of a verse in the Psalms," he said. "The verse is Psalm 115:3, 'But our God is in the heavens; He hath done whatsoever He hath pleased' (KJV)."

Growing increasingly more puzzled, I nodded.

He continued, "Your mother just called. Dad is in the hospital with acute leukemia. The doctors . . . " and his voice broke. "You have reservations on a plane leaving in two hours. I have already arranged for Lynn to be cared for."

Then he put his arms around me and held me tight.

I was numb. Yet strangely not unprepared. A few weeks before, God had impressed a verse on my heart as

I was reading His Word, which said, "He shall not be afraid of evil tidings; his heart is fixed, trusting in the Lord" (Psalm 112:7, KJV). I felt God was telling me that something was going to happen soon for which I needed to be spiritually prepared. However, I hadn't dreamed that my robust 57-year-old father would be stricken.

Two hours later I was on a plane eastward bound. Finances prevented Jack from accompanying me, and I felt very much alone.

The next 10 days blurred together. Daddy grew worse rapidly, caught pneumonia, and died five days after my arrival. The burial arrangements, the funeral, the grief, the sustaining grace of God, His comfort and peace, packing, bringing Mother back to the coast with me all telescoped together through the lens of sorrow.

Then I was home. Jack met us, and after getting Mother settled in the guest room, he took me out in our little VW. Parking in a quiet spot off the road, he turned to comfort me.

An unbidden thought flashed through my mind. *How can you comfort me?* it grumbled. *You weren't there. You can't know what I've been through. You can't really understand.* And my heart was cold. I pulled the tattered edges of my grief to me and hugged them in loneliness and self-pity.

But God would not allow it. In one brief second, I had to make a choice—to shut Jack out because I thought he couldn't totally understand or to share this thing together.

Deliberately, by an act of my will, I put my wounded spirit in the hands of Jack's concern to be bandaged with his love.

Many forks occur in our marriage roads—choices which lead us together or tear us apart. Later, I realized this was one of them—the *sharing* of pain, sorrow, and grief, or the *shutting out* of the other because I thought he could not understand completely.

At Lynn's birth, Jack couldn't actually feel the bearing down pains as I labored to bring her into the world, but he shared them. I couldn't have made it through those 48 hours without his strength and comfort. In one way, I think he suffered more than I.

The intense pain that bathed his body in perspiration within seconds after a kidney stone attack made me want to writhe in empathy, but all I could do was race him to the hospital. He bore the pain, but we shared the experience.

That's what it is all about. Choosing to share and to understand.

But it isn't *easy* to understand.

One of Charles Schulz' Peanuts cartoons illustrates our dilemma.[1]

I have to sympathize with Charlie Brown. We have so much understanding to do that I sometimes feel "I don't even understand what it is I don't understand."

All of us view others from a biased point of view. We can't help comparing another's actions and responses with how we would have acted or responded. When we fail to see things through another's eyes, when we have no understanding, then inevitably a *different* response than our own would be comes out a *wrong* response.

J. B. Phillips paraphrases Ephesians 4:32 this way: "Be kind to one another; be understanding. Be as ready to forgive others as God for Christ's sake has forgiven you."

Be kind.

Be understanding.

Be forgiving. Not just a little forgiving. But as much as God for Christ's sake has already forgiven you. How much is that? Everything. Totally.

A good marriage is simply the union of "two awfully good forgivers." Yet forgiveness is hard. One man said, "When we quarrel, my wife becomes historical." His friend replied, "Don't you mean hysterical?" "No," the first replied, "I mean historical. She reminds me of everything I ever did to her." To forgive is to put the offense away completely. Real forgiveness requires strength and love from God.

But directly in the middle of this verse in Ephesians in the Phillips paraphrase, between kindness and forgiveness, comes the phrase, "Be understanding."

Most of us have little or no real understanding of one another. And it takes a "heap of understanding" to make a marriage.

It is a lifelong project to learn to understand each other. But only in understanding is true love. If you can figure out the person with whom you are living, everything else will be easy by comparison.

I have to understand Jack's background, his idiosyncrasies, his introvert leanings, his personality, how he views and interacts with the world around him, his thinking. He has to do the same with me. To know him that completely, I have to study him.

Mrs. Norman Vincent Peale puts her finger right on this area:

If I could give one piece of advice to young brides, and only one, it would be this: study your man. Study him as if he were some rare and strange and fascinating animal, which he is. Study his likes and dislikes, his strengths and weaknesses, his moods and mannerisms. Just loving a man is fine, but it's not enough. To live with one successfully you have to know him, and to know him, you have to study him.

Look around you and decide how many of the best marriages you know are ones where a wife in a deep sense actually knows her husband better than he knows himself. Knows what pleases him. Knows what upsets him. Knows what makes him laugh or makes him angry. Knows when he needs encouragement. Knows when he's too charged up about something and needs to be held back. Knows, in other words, exactly what makes him tick.[2]

For years I never really *studied* Jack. I was much like the bride of seven weeks I talked with a while ago. It had been a hectic two weeks for her and she felt they really were not communicating. At last they had a few moments alone one Sunday afternoon and were lying on the bed with her head on his shoulder.

After a long, poignant silence, she asked, "What are you thinking?" (Men, if your wife ever asks you that question in those circumstances, *please* be thinking about her.)

This one wasn't. Instead, his choice answer was, "Oh, I was just wondering what I should tell the boss tomorrow when he asks me about that project I've been working on."

She said, "Oh!"

Then she waited. Now any man with a grain of knowledge about the working of most women's minds would have known she was waiting for him to ask *her* what *she* was thinking.

This one didn't. Instead, he asked, "Are you going to fix supper pretty soon?"

Between clenched teeth she flatly monotoned, "Maybe in a little while."

"Well," he offered cheerily, "I'll be glad to teach you how to fix cheese-dogs."

With that innocent offer, the lid blew off her anger. He thought, *What did I say to make her so angry? She is being unreasonable!*

She thought, *This man I married doesn't have the sensitivity of a frog!*

This bride related that incident to me several weeks after it happened. She had never told her husband what was really on her mind that Sunday afternoon. As a result of this one incident, their marriage very quickly had begun going in two directions—his way and her way, 180° away from each other. She was getting angry more often because she felt totally misunderstood. He continued thinking he had married an unhappy and frustrated woman.

My friend needed one of three things to handle that situation, if not all three. She needed humor, to laugh at herself, at him, at the situation (but a bride of seven weeks seldom can do that).

Or, she needed openness, to be able to say honestly, "Hey, that hurt. I wanted you to be thinking about me, because I'm feeling romantic right now and quite vulnerable because we haven't had a chance to talk the last two weeks."

Or, she needed to understand that her husband was put together on a quite different frequency than she. When he was thinking about business instead of thinking about her, it was not a sign that he didn't love her deeply (which was the first thing that came to her mind).

My friend had neither humor, nor openness, nor understanding. Like me in those early years, she had not begun to *study* her husband.

True understanding is a lifelong project. A day . . . a week . . . a year of study will not suffice. The rich reward of deep sharing, clear understanding, total love is won only by devoting an entire life to praying and working toward those goals. Each of us is constantly changing. Study that change with wonder. Determine with God's help to *choose to understand*.

NOTES: 1. Copyright 1971 by United Feature Syndicate, Inc. Used by permission.
2. Mrs. Norman Vincent Peale, *The Adventure of Being a Wife* (Englewood Cliffs, New Jersey: Prentice-Hall, Inc., 1971), page 29.

5

CHOOSING TO KNOW
by Carole

JACK and Carole Mayhall.
Color us different.
Color Jack's hair red. Frost it with gray. Paint on eyes—deep brown.

Color Carole's eyes blue, speckled with green. Hair: brown. (Please paint out the gray.)

But don't stop with the outward.

Peel off the surface layers and color us totally different inside too. Through the years the colors have muted and blended in some areas of personality. But they will forever be individual.

Vive la difference!

God gave us two eyes to see things from a slightly different point of view. If we have only one eye, we lose perspective. We see things flat, rather than round. We lose some of the wonder of the world around us.

God created couples with slightly different points of view for the same reason. We will have a better view of the world, a better understanding of people, and more perspective if we use both points of view.

But to *use* our differences, we have to understand them, and then to accept them. As we talk to couples, we find very few who have begun to do this. Our differences, accepted and appreciated, are God's way of making us *fit* together as a couple. So that we will be stronger together than either of us could be apart. Jack's strengths compensate for my weaknesses and my gifts supplement areas in which he is lacking. As some of our differences are explained, God's creativity in distinctives is evident.

Jack is an objective person. To him a fact is a fact is a fact is a fact. He often takes a detached view of life and his perspective is broad. He thinks in concepts rather than in particulars.

Not me. I have a difficult time being objective or detached about *anything*. From my point of view, a fact is never a cold, hard fact, but a little bit more than or a fraction less than a fact depending on my frame of mind.

There is one big hole in the fabric of Jack's objectivity, however, and that hole is *me*. He can turn subjective in a split second when I come on in a negative way concerning something he has said or done. Because I love him, I need to understand this exception. I need to be sensitive to his sensitivity.

With my subjective nature, I take teasing very poorly. Even if Jack grins reassuringly when he calls me "Chubby" (*if* he calls me "Chubby"), I will be positive he is telling me I am immersed in rolls of fat. And even if that were true, I couldn't take being reminded by a barb even if it was in jest.

If Jack remarks, "The Joneses are busy and can't come tomorrow," I'll think, *I wonder if we've offended them?*

I even identify with this incident where subjectiveness borders on the ridiculous.

A man said to his wife, "Honey, you've been working so hard all week, cooking, cleaning, and taking care of the kids. Tonight I'm going to take you out for a good dinner."

And his wife burst into tears!

For you who didn't get it, she had picked up on the "*good* dinner." What had she been cooking for him all week? Bad meals? Earlier in my married life, I could have been seriously hurt by a kind, generous offer such as that one. Not any more. Now I realize that Jack would be making a thoughtful offer and would in no way be making a derogatory remark about the nature of my meals.

Knowing my own nature helps me work on being more understanding and at trying to take a more objective approach. But often when my head tells me not to take something personally, my heart still says, "Ouch!" I am now trying to get my heart and my head all connected up right.

Jack, on the other hand, understands my emotions better all the time. He tries to be very careful about teasing and I appreciate him for it. I have to accept Jack's objectivity and he has to accept my subjective nature. Neither are wrong; they are just different. But we have to *know* these things about one another.

Another big difference in us is that I have a mind which grooves on details while Jack goes right to the essential point of a matter. This has many implications in our relationship. It has caused me to feel he wasn't interested in my conversation, wasn't interested in telling me about his job, and even, at times, made me feel he wasn't interested in *people*. None of which are true.

Often he would go to a week-long conference and, on arriving home, find me waiting to hear *all* about it. So he would tell me all about it—in 10 minutes flat. I would think, *He doesn't care enough to tell me about the conference.* Yet from his point of view, he had told me *all* about that conference. He had zeroed in on the essential points of the week. I had wanted to hear all the details. We both ended up frustrated and sometimes angry due to different thinking processes.

I am learning that it is so much more important to think *together* than to think *alike*. We are different. We will always remain so. We are learning to accept and understand these differences. I am no longer hurt when he tells me all about a conference in 10 minutes. (However, I have learned how to ask the right questions to ferret out details that I want to know. And he has learned to jot down who is going to have babies, who is engaged, and what was the best meal he had.)

Being detail-minded helps me to do several things at once. I can be cooking lasagna, talking on the telephone, letting the dog out, and planning a party all at the same time. Jack's concentration is distracted by interruptions as he concentrates on one thing at a time. Not wrong. Just different.

Have you ever started to tell a man like Jack about your next door neighbor, the one whose husband ran for the Senate, whose secretary was divorced last year . . . you know, the one who had the maiden aunt who was in a sanitorium for a while last year, and . . . ? Suddenly you glance at your husband and his eyes are glazed over and sort of crossed. You think, *He's not listening to me.* And you are right. You lost him four details ago.

Before I understood more of Jack's thinking processes, at this point I would think, *Oh, if he isn't listening, then he's not interested. If he's not interested in what I am saying, he must not be interested in* me. *Therefore, how could he love* me *the way I long to be loved?*

Consciously or subconsciously, my mind works that way. Criticism, inference, even a difference of opinion can set my mind on my own private pilgrimage which ends with, *He must not love me the way I long to be loved.* I need constant reassurance of Jack's love, which fortunately he understands and gives me.

My mind for details leads me to be impressed by and often distracted by a lot of little things—the accidental and the incidental. Jack will say, "That's a good-looking car, but how does it run?" (the essential)

I'll say, "I just don't care for the color" (the detail).

Jack may say, "This is a well-constructed house."

And I will comment, "The view from the bedroom is spectacular."

Jack looks at how new the furnace is.

I notice the color of the living room rug.

Jack looks for storm windows, while I admire the bathroom wallpaper. Jack checks the insulation, and I appreciate the paneling. Not wrong. Just different.

Now before you wonder how we've managed to stay together for so many years, I want to show how beautifully God fit Jack and me together, to make us *stronger* and for us to help each other.

It has been said that "intuition" is more than a feeling with no basis. Someone has suggested that it is rather a mind for detail which gives birth to a feeling.

Jack and I can go into a situation and have different vibes about it. When we come away, often he asks how I *felt* about it. When I tell him, he shakes his head in wonder. But a great many times I'm right.

What has happened? I have picked up 20 little details that I am unaware of noticing—a tone of voice, a raised eyebrow, a posture. They have been filtered into the computer of my mind and come back to me as a feeling, an intuition if you will. Jack takes that feeling, filters it through his objective grid, and investigates. He comes away with a much better perspective than if either of us saw that situation alone. We *fit* together.

Jack needs my detail-oriented mind, and I certainly need his ability to see the essentials and to be objective in situations where I respond emotionally. I can sense how people are reacting faster than Jack can and he uses this.

Jack tends to be much more logical in his thinking process. He will study the evidence and, in a step-by-step reasoning process, reach a conclusion. I rely much more on intuition, instinct, and emotion to reach the conclusion, many times the same one (and my way is faster, too).

I was talking to a friend of mine who said she was going to sign up for a course in conversation. When I asked her why she was planning to take such a course, as she is an enthusiastic, interesting person already, she said her husband gets angry at her for not "talking straight." He says she doesn't say what she *means* in a direct way.

I wished her luck with the course, and told her if it worked, I'd join the next one.

I am most grateful for a husband who doesn't get irritated at the way I think and talk.

Jack, being logical, thinks in straight lines and talks that way too; direct, to the point, no frills. I think more in circles, and talk in circles at times as well. Now this is something I am working on, but in which I will never be proficient. I'm sure it has something to do with the sensitivity part of me. In other words, unless I sneak up on a subject, rather than hitting it head-on, I might get hurt . . . or hurt you. For instance, you might hear the following conversation around our house 15 minutes before we are to go out to dinner.

Carole: I suppose I really ought to change.
Jack: Well, why don't you? (Zoom! To the point!)
Carole: Don't you like what I've got on?
Jack: It's OK, but you said you were going to change.
Carole: I was just saying that to see if it was alright not to.
Jack: (Looks baffled and shakes his head.)

It is complicated living with most of us. I even had trouble understanding *me.*

All mixed up in the above is the way Jack and I use speech. Jack speaks to convey facts and ideas. I often use speech to express a feeling or an emotion. This was vital to learn about one another. Not to understand this causes many moments of despair.

One evening Jack and I were looking at a full, lovely moon. It was an incredibly beautiful evening, and I said, "Isn't that a beautiful moon?"

What was I really saying? Jack could see the moon. I certainly wasn't pointing it out to him. What I was really saying was this, "This beautiful evening with that full moon makes me feel very romantic!"

When Jack answered, "Yes, it is bright enough to shoot a golf ball by," he grinned very quickly so I knew he was kidding, or I would have dissolved into tears. We had been married long enough by that time for him to pick up my feeling and to respond to it.

If it is raining outside and I look out and say, "Oh, it is raining," I could be expressing a number of things, most of them *feelings.* I could mean that the rain makes me feel depressed, or it makes me feel energetic, like cleaning house.

If Jack says, "It's raining outside," he is simply saying that the heavens have parted and little drops of moisture are falling to the ground. He is expressing a fact. I am expressing a feeling.

I backed the car out of the garage one day, turning too sharply and taking a piece of the garage along with the fender. I rushed into the house and said, "Oh, I feel just terrible! You can't imagine how awful it was to hear that 'crunch' and . . . "

Jack interrupted, "Never mind that. What happened?"

If that incident had happened a few years before it did, I would have been completely crushed, thinking that Jack was either angry at me, or didn't care whether I was alright or not, or didn't understand. I probably would have cried most of the afternoon. The incident would have triggered that old thought pattern of "he doesn't care how I'm feeling. If he doesn't care about my feelings, he doesn't care about me and he can't love me the way I want to be loved." It could have been days before I got back to the proper perspective.

Instead, I thought, *Oh, yes, he is interested in the facts. He will listen to my feelings later.* And it was alright because I knew he would listen. And he did.

I want to understand. And in that understanding, accept. But I need the wisdom of God to do that. And I need the God of Wisdom. Often I pray, "Lord, help Jack and me fall more in love with each other. Help us understand each other. Help me accept him. Help us become, as a couple, more than we ever could as individuals."

A poem by Roy Croft sums up my feelings:

I love you,
Not only for what you are
But for what I am
When I am with you.

I love you,
Not only for what
You have made of yourself
But for what
You are making of me.

I love you,
For the part of me
That you bring out;
I love you
For putting your hand
Into my heaped-up heart
And passing over
All the foolish, weak things
That you can't help
Dimly seeing there,
And for drawing out
Into the light
All the beautiful belongings
That no one else had looked
Quite far enough to find.

I love you because you
Are helping me to make
Of the lumber of my life
Not a tavern
But a temple;
Out of works
Of my every day
Not a reproach
But a song.[1]

NOTES: 1. Roy Croft, "I Love You."

6

CHOOSING TO ADJUST
by Jack

Scene: Christmas at the Mayhalls
Characters: All the relatives who can be gathered from far and wide
Action: By candlelight the Christmas story is read, voices join in singing the old familiar carols, and prayers of worship and thanksgiving go up to the Lord
Finally: The gifts. One person at a time chooses a gift, presents it to the receiver who, after opening it, takes his turn in selecting another gift. (With all the thank-yous and try-ons, this can take several hours.)

OBSERVING this occasion, you just might be overwhelmed by all the love and affection around our tree. You never saw so much hugging and kissing in your life. At least, I hadn't when I first joined that crowd.

In my family, such exuberant demonstrations of affection were rare. I knew that my mother and dad loved each other and my sister and me, but it was demonstrated differently from the profuse hugging and kissing that went on in Carole's clan. In her family, everybody kissed everybody for no apparent reason.

Every Christmas I am reminded of the need we have to understand and accept each other's family backgrounds and the results of that background on our wives and husbands. Not only are we to understand and accept, but we must adjust to one another where that needs to be done. In the case of the joyously unrestrained affection . . . well, I'd have been a fool if I had stifled *that* in Carole. So I was the one who did most of the adjusting, and I began to express love more openly than I did as a child in my own home. I really like all that hugging and kissing now.

What about celebrating holidays? That seems like a simple thing, doesn't it? Yet we have talked to couples who have let a gulf develop in their relationship simply because of the difference in how they were used to celebrating special occasions. Women in whose families birthdays were celebrated with gifts and parties marry men whose families ignored the whole affair. Men whose tradition was a giant picnic-reunion on Labor Day for every cousin around marry women whose idea of Labor Day is to labor.

Husbands who think doing the dishes is unmanly marry women whose fathers always helped in the kitchen. Women who grew up having a cup of coffee for breakfast marry a man who grows faint unless he has steak, eggs, potatoes, and toast.

These couples never thought to discuss such issues before marriage, of course. And they never took the time afterward. So irritations arose simply because they had not discussed how *they* as a couple wanted to celebrate or not celebrate special days, and how the two of *them* wanted to handle daily chores, habits of eating, sleeping, and living.

To communicate concerning these family differences

in our backgrounds is vital. To choose to understand and accept them is imperative.

Another difference that needs to be explored and understood between a couple is the introvert/extrovert difference. If I were to identify the two of us, I would say that Carole tends to be more extrovertish and I would lean toward the introvert side of the scale. I am more quiet, reserved, and conservative. My wife is bubbly, outgoing, effervescent, and vivacious.

A young couple visited us one summer for an overnight stay. As the husband and I were sitting at the breakfast table drinking our second cups of coffee, he got rather serious and asked if he could pose a personal question. I told him to go ahead.

He said, "Jack, I've noticed that your wife and my wife are quite a bit alike [and he mentioned these things I have just stated about Carole], and I have noticed that you and I are somewhat alike." (He then described us as tending toward the introvertish side.) Then he asked me this significant question: "How do you handle that problem?"

I asked, "What problem?"

To me, this was not a problem. I honestly can't remember if it was in our early years of marriage. But God has taught us to blend together and work as a team rather than competing with one another. This man's attitude toward his wife's *personality* was that it was a problem because her personality was a threat to him. Being more quiet and reserved, he was somewhat intimidated by crowds which were absolutely no threat to his outgoing wife. While he was uncomfortable, she was at ease. Instead of seeing this as an asset, he looked on it as a liability. To him, then, it was a problem.

Our God is creative. When he fits two people together, He can and will give insight as to the blending together of, and the capitalizing on, each other's strengths. *If we ask Him.* In the case of Carole's and my personalities, God has shown me how to use this asset in my wife.

For instance, I hate small talk. When I find myself in a situation where the talk centers around the weather or last week's football game, I can take it only so long and then my mind begins to wander. I try to look intelligent and attentive, as though I am taking in the entire conversation. Looking me straight in the eye, you'd think I was grasping everything that was being said. But my wife looks at me and knows that my mind may be 1,000 miles away. When she recognizes that certain look in my eyes, she picks up the conversation ball, carries it, fields any questions that are thrown my way, and nobody knows the difference. Now that's a tremendous asset!

Another difference which will sometimes ferment is when a perfectionist lives with one who is not. I tend to be a perfectionist. Carole tends to be, not exactly sloppy, but *fast.*

Without realizing it at first, this started to cause problems in our early days of marriage. My tendency was, "If you can't do it right, don't do it." Consequently, I would procrastinate on many occasions because I didn't have the time to do it right. On the other hand, Carole would jump right into a project and get it done, sometimes not the way I would have liked it.

In this, we have learned not only to accept, but also how to adjust to one another. I learned that with some jobs, it *was* important that they get done more sooner than later, even if the job was not perfectly done. Conversely, Carole has learned that some jobs need to be given more time to do thoroughly. We are both better for the adjusting and are learning to operate as a team to accomplish more than we could alone.

Solomon puts it this way, "Iron sharpens iron, so one man sharpens another" (Proverbs 27:17). In a real sense, God can take a husband and wife and use them to polish and hone each other into diamonds that will better reflect Jesus Christ.

Four steps of action need to be taken to defuse any potential explosive situation:

1. Know your mate—study her/him so that you get to know her/him well.
2. Understand your mate—this has to do with communication. Get things out in the open and talk about them. It also needs prayer—asking God for the wisdom to understand the person to whom you are married.
3. Adjust to your mate—this has to do with a willingness and openness on your part to change and adjust together so that you truly *do* fit together.
4. Accept your mate—this is an important aspect of love.

Know, understand, adjust, and accept. These are choices we have to make.

7

CHOOSING TO FORGIVE
by Carole

SHE LOOKED at me defiantly. Hope, hurt, pain, and anger were mingled in her eyes and in her tone as she said, "I can't do it, Carole. Could you?"

I shook my head. She had just told me her problem —and it was a giant one. Her in-laws had physically and verbally attacked her in front of her husband and children. And her husband had not only failed to come to her defense, but had sided with his parents. How could she forgive such a thing?

"No," I replied, "*I* couldn't forgive him. But *God* can—and will through and in you, if you'll let Him. There is no hope for your marriage if you *don't* forgive."

I could have added that there would be no hope for *her*, either. The lack of forgiveness produces a poison that will eat away one's very existence, especially the existence of any joy or peace in our lives.

What heartache!

I have talked with women who have been subjected to beatings, infidelities, and unnatural sexual acts by their husbands; and I've talked with husbands who have had their trust betrayed. How can a person forgive such sins?

There is no easy answer. But this I know. God *does* have a solution. It is somehow tied up with the solemn warning: "Looking diligently lest any man fail of the grace of God, lest any root of bitterness springing up trouble you, and thereby many be defiled" (Hebrews 12:15, KJV). What does "fail of the grace of God" mean? One translation puts it, "Comes short of the grace of God" (NASB); and I would paraphrase it, "Fails to receive enough of the grace of God."

If we don't have enough of His grace, it isn't God's fault. His grace *is* sufficient for our every need (2 Corinthians 12:9). The fault is ours because we haven't really *asked* for His grace with an accepting heart.

What is forgiveness? The dictionary defines *forgive* as: "To cease to feel resentment against (an offender): pardon . . . to give up resentment of or claim to requital for . . to grant relief from payment of."[1]

I was struck with two things about this definition. First, was the *feeling* involved—"to cease *to feel* resentment." This statement rules out such remarks as, "I forgive him, but I can't forget it," or, "I forgive him in my head, but not in my heart." If we cease to feel resentment, our hearts are free.

Many times we don't really want to forgive, for if we forgive, we become vulnerable to be hurt all over again. So we build our walls of resentment and unforgiveness in order not to feel pain again. Logically this makes some kind of sense. But emotionally it is deadly poison. And it poisons the person with the unforgiving heart first of all. When a person hardens his or her feelings against pain, *all* feeling can be deadened.

I have met many wives who are unable to respond physically to their husbands, and with some of them the reason stems from an unforgiving heart. One wife resented the fact that she had to give up her career as a nurse when she married. She had buried the resentment against her unsuspecting husband to the point that she was unaware that it was there. But she was totally unresponsive physically. When God uncovered her resentment, when it was brought out in the open, confessed, and forgiven, feeling flowed back into the sexual union of her marriage.

The second thing that struck me about Webster's definition was the verbs used for the three statements: *cease, give up,* and *grant.* An act of our wills is involved in our *ceasing* to feel resentful, in *giving up* a claim for payment, and in *granting* or extending to the offender relief from payment. But to do this is not easy.

David Augsburger, radio speaker for "The Mennonite Hour," puts it this way:

> Forgiveness is hard. Especially in a marriage tense with past troubles, tormented by fears of rejection and humiliation, and torn by suspicion and distrust.
>
> Forgiveness hurts. Especially when it must be extended to a husband or wife who doesn't deserve it, who hasn't earned it, who may misuse it. It hurts to forgive.
>
> Forgiveness costs. Especially in marriage when it means accepting instead of demanding repayment for the wrong done; where it means releasing the other instead of exacting revenge; where it means reaching out in love instead of relinquishing resentments. It costs to forgive.[2]

He later explains that . . .

> stated psychologically, forgiveness takes place when the person who was offended and justly angered by the offender bears his own anger, and lets the other go free.

Anger cannot be ignored, denied, or forgotten without doing treachery in hidden ways. It must be dealt with responsibly, honestly, in a decisive act of the will. Either the injured and justifiably angry person vents his feelings on the other in retaliation—(that is an attempt at achieving justice as accuser, judge, and hangman all in one)—or the injured person may choose to accept his angry feelings, bear the burden of them personally, find release through confession and prayer and set the other person free. This is forgiveness.[3]

This is what Jesus Christ did for us. He forgave us unconditionally, bearing the burden, setting us free. "In Him we have redemption through His blood, the forgiveness of our trespasses, according to the riches of His grace, which He lavished upon us" (Ephesians 1:7-8; see 1 Peter 2:24).

The degree to which we are able to forgive others is the degree to which we can be open to the love of Jesus in our lives. Do you remember who hurt you last year? I have a friend who remembers every negative thing anyone has ever said about her. For the past twenty years she has written it all down in a little book. Jesus said, "And whenever you stand praying, you *must* forgive anything that you are holding against anyone else, and your Heavenly Father will forgive you your sins." (Mark 11:25, PH).[4]

Most of us do not deal with giant things that we need to forgive. Many times it is the little, picky matters which stick in our throats and cause us to choke. When we do not deal with the seemingly inconsequential things, we fail to "walk in the light." The Apostle John said, "If we walk in the light as He Himself is in the light, we have fellowship with one another, and the blood of Jesus His Son cleanses us from all sin" (1 John 1:7).

Are you walking in the light with your mate? In Christ there is *no darkness at all*, no hidden, secret resentment, no anger or self-pity or criticism. If we are walking in the light *as He is in the light*, then we will really have fellowship with one another. We will be best friends in open, honest sharing.

Question: How long should you allow a resentment to linger?

Answer: You should not let it stay a day or an hour or a moment. As long as that resentment, that bitterness lies in your heart, you are failing to "walk in the light."

We must forgive and forgive immediately.

Stated in marriage relationships, forgiveness takes place when love accepts—deliberately—the hurts and abrasions of life and drops all charges against the other person. Forgiveness is accepting the other when both of you know he or she has done something unacceptable.

Forgiveness is smiling silent love to your partner when the justifications for keeping an insult or injury alive are on the tip of your tongue, yet you swallow them. Not because you have to, to keep peace, but because you want to, to make peace.

Forgiveness is not acceptance given "on condition" that the other become acceptable. Forgiveness is given freely. Out of a keen awareness that the forgiver also has been of constant forgiveness, daily.

Forgiveness exercises God's strength to love and receive the other person without any assurance of complete restitution and making of amends.

Forgiveness is a relationship between equals who recognize their deep need of each other, share and share alike. Each needs the other's forgiveness. Each needs the other's acceptance. Each needs the other.[5]

NOTES: 1. By permission. From *Webster's New Collegiate Dictionary.* © 1977 by G. & C. Merriam Co., Publishers of the Merriam-Webster Dictionaries, page 451.
2. David W. Augsburger, *Cherishable: Love and Marriage* (Scottsdale, Pennsylvania: Herald Press, 1971), pages 141-142.
3. *Cherishable: Love and Marriage,* page 144.
4. From *Discovering How to Pray* by Hope MacDonald, page 69. Copyright © 1976 by The Zondervan Corporation, Grand Rapids, Michigan. Used by permission.
5. *Cherishable: Love and Marriage,* page 146.

SECTION III

Communication

8

CHOOSING TO CLARIFY
by Carole

I AM constantly amazed at the insights of Charles Schulz in his Peanuts cartoon strip. One Sunday I both laughed and sighed at the frustration of poor Charlie Brown as I read the following:

Peppermint Patty: Explain love to me, Chuck.

Charlie Brown: You can't explain love . . . I can recommend a book, or a painting, or a song, or a poem, but I can't explain love.

PP: Try, Chuck! Try to explain love . . .

CB: Well, say I happen to see this cute little girl walk by, and I . . .

PP: Why does she have to be cute, Chuck? Can't someone fall in love with a girl who isn't cute, and has freckles and a big nose? Explain *that*, Chuck!!

CB: Well, maybe you're right . . . Let's just say, then, that I happen to see this girl walk by who has a great big nose, and . . .

PP (yelling):   I didn't say a great big nose, Chuck!
CB (flat on his back):   You not only can't explain love . . .
actually, you can't even talk about
it . . . [1]

Charlie Brown had difficulty communicating on a complex topic like love. For many of us, talking about ordinary subjects even seems unattainable. Nancy Stahl tells of one such incident.

Every once in a while, I become a bit broody over the fact that my role as an exotic enchantress has become something of a bit part.

Not that I expect my husband's nostrils to flare whenever the hem of my skirt brushes his knee. I don't even expect him to quiver with erotic delight when I scratch the place on his back where he can never reach.

But I have the uncomfortable feeling every morning that if I greeted him at the door stark raving naked, he would tell me that I had lipstick on my teeth.

What I object to most is that, unless one counts the sparkling one-sided conversations I carry on with the dog, the cryptic remarks I address to the washing machine, and an occasional chat with Dial-a-Prayer, I spend ten hours of every day virtually incommunicado. By evening I am sobbingly eager to be recognized as the gay, witty nymph I really am and to perhaps engage in a spot of repartee.

"How was your day?" I began last night, addressing my opening gambit to the back of the sports page.

"Umm."

"Did you have a good lunch?"

"Umm."

"I'm having the roof reshingled with gold-plated clam shells," I remarked casually.

"Ummhummm."

"The TV repairman is madly in love with me. We're running off together next Wednesday morning right after I get back from Weight Watchers."

"Umm."

"Talk to me!" I finally shrieked. He stared at me as if I had just demanded that he shave his legs.

"I've *been* talking to you."

"You haven't been talking, you've been umming. You haven't heard a word I've said," I complained.

"I've heard everything you've said," he argued. "By the way, you have lipstick on your teeth."[2]

Dwight Small, pastor and marriage counselor, has said, "How suddenly holy wedlock can become unholy deadlock!"[3] And this is true. Our marriages are either duels or duets, sometimes both, depending on when you look in. Only God has the answers to help us continually sing a duet instead of waging duels. We may not always listen to His answers, but He most certainly has them.

We cannot expect the wages of happiness if we do not work for them. One of the most difficult jobs is to achieve depth in our communication.

J. A. Fritze, a Lutheran minister and clinical counselor, has said, "You can't know anyone unless you communicate with them. You can't love anything you don't know. Therefore, the depth of love existing between a husband and wife will largely depend on the amount and *depth* of their communication."[4]

Communication—the right kind of communication—is probably the most vital ingredient in the success of our marriages. Love cannot exist without it.

It is true that it is impossible *not* to communicate. We

speak volumes when we refuse to say a word. The shouts of silence are heard very clearly. But what they are saying gets jumbled in the receiving. When a husband is silent, most wives feel it is because he doesn't care. When wives are silent, many men feel they are angry. Even if our assumptions were correct, silence does not help these matters.

A simple definition of communication is that it is "a process, (either verbal or non-verbal) of sharing information with another person in such a way that he *understands* what you are saying."[5] The key is the *understanding*. If a person clearly understands why one is *not* talking, it may be all right. Usually however, silence is interpreted incorrectly, and cloudy, unclear messages are received.

In the last few years, Jack and I have learned a great deal about clarifying meaning . . . hard work for me. I am adept at circling issues, going off into tangents to try to make a point, coding my messages and hoping Jack can decode them. I seldom reach my goal of consistently "saying what I mean and meaning what I say." But this *is* my goal. I shoot for it, because as the saying goes, "If you aim at nothing, you are bound to hit it." My goal, my aim is to clarify meaning and to say what I mean. It is a lifetime project.

Remember, it is more important to think *together* than to think *alike*. Jack and I will *never* think alike, and that's fine. To bring two different ways of thinking together adds perspective and strength to our marriage. We have to learn to bring our wavelengths together constantly so that we are continually understanding one another. The most helpful way that we have found to do this is by asking questions such as, "What do you mean?" "What are you really saying?" "This is how I'm taking what you have just said," and rephrasing the statement. We have been amazed that even after many years of living together, we still misunderstand the other's meaning unless we clarify often in this way.

Communication specialists tell us that there are six messages involved in the communication process:

1. What you mean to say.
2. What you actually say.
3. What the other person hears.
4. What the other person thinks he hears.
5. What the other person says about what you said.
6. What you think the other person said about what you said.[6]

Gets a bit complicated, doesn't it?

In Chapter 5, I mentioned an incident when Jack and I were looking at a gorgeous moon together under romantic circumstances. As we shared that moment, how was I actually feeling? I was feeling romantic. If we followed the six messages, that incident would have looked something like this:

1. What you mean to say.	"The moon puts me in a romantic mood."
2. What you actually say.	"Isn't that a brilliant moon?"
3. What the other person hears.	"The moon is bright."
4. What the other person thinks he hears.	"The moon is bright enough for a walk."
5. What the other person says about what you said.	"Yes, it's bright enough to shoot a golf ball by."

6. What you think the   "I don't feel romantic."
other person said about
what you said.

We can miss each other's wavelengths completely by the time the six messages are completed without even realizing what has happened. All of us are constantly in the process of coding and decoding messages. We can't avoid this, though it is something we must work on. For instance, Jack may come home from work and ask a simple question, such as, "When is dinner?"

I could interpret his question as: "I'm very hungry. Could you hurry dinner so we can eat right away?"

I would be entirely wrong. Jack is a jogger and likes to run before dinner several times a week. So what he could be asking is, "Do I have time to run before dinner, or are you cooking something that can't wait?"

Because we have been working on "saying what we mean," he is more frequently asking, "Do I have time to run before dinner?" which is not a coded message. But when he doesn't clarify, I need to say, "Do you want to run before dinner or are you especially hungry and want me to hurry it up?"

Being much more logical and factual than I am, Jack doesn't send as many ambiguous messages as I do. And he is getting adept at decoding my confusing messages. But now when I hear myself sending a complicated verbal thought, I am more likely to catch myself and state it more clearly. I'll say, "I guess what I am really trying to say . . ." and clarify. But because I am the kind of person I am, I know I'll never do this perfectly, nor will any of us for that matter. So we need to learn to ask questions, or restate the point for clarification of meaning.

On a visit to England, we had a delightful day with

some friends. Driving along the freeway, Jeannie suddenly said, "It's five o'clock." Now all of us had watches. We were aware of the time. Obviously that statement held more than was on the surface. We laughed and said, "OK, Jeannie, what are you *really* saying?"

What she was *really* saying to her husband was, "Do I have time to go home and check up on the children before we go out for dinner?" But I wonder if we hadn't asked her to clarify, would she have gone through that entire evening worrying about her children and frustrated because we had failed to pick up her meaning?

We are proficient at dropping small coded gems into our conversations. If someone doesn't pick up the signals, we may be wounded without that person even being aware of our hurt. It is surely unfair, and immature. But most of us expect others to carry around a burdensome "unscrambler" for our coded messages.

To say what we mean, and say it *straight*, must be our constant goal in order for those around us to be able to discard all decoding devices.

NOTES: 1. Text from PEANUTS by Charles M. Schulz; © 1975 by United Feature Syndicate, Inc. Used by permission.
2. Nancy Stahl, *Jelly Side Down,* pages 46-47. (Greenwich, Connecticut: Fawcett Publications, Inc., 1972. Copyright © 1970, 1971 by Universal Press Syndicate, used by permission.)
3. Dwight Hervey Small, *Design for Christian Marriage* (Westwood, New Jersey: Fleming H. Revell Company, 1959), page 53.
4. From *The Essence of Marriage* by Julius Fritze, page 65. Copyright © 1969 by Zondervan Publishing House.
5. H. Norman Wright, *Communication, Key to Your Marriage* (Glendale, California: Regal Books, 1974), page 53.
6. *Communication, Key to Your Marriage,* page 54.

9

CHOOSING TO LISTEN
by Carole

WE HAD dinner with a young couple one evening, and their conversation reminded me of a verbal tennis match. The problem was that they were not playing the game with each other. It was more like they were playing with different tennis ball machines.

He started in on a topic of interest to him. She interrupted and took off on another track. A moment later, he interrupted her and went back to his original subject. She then broke in on him, and on and on it went.

The most startling thing about this conversation, if you can call it that, was that they were totally unaware of what they were doing. It had become an ingrained pattern with them.

It has been said that listening intently with one's mouth completely and firmly shut is a basic communication skill needed in all marriages. Most of us are so concerned about getting our own ideas across that we only concentrate on the talking aspect of the conversation. We talk *to* people, not *with* them. In doing this, we fail to listen to the other person.

The story is told of a little boy who came to his mother and asked, "Mommy, where did I come from?"

Having heard that when children are old enough to ask that question, they should be told, she thought, *Here goes*, and proceeded to explain the whole complicated process of reproduction. The boy got more and more puzzled throughout her monolog.

When she had finally finished her dissertation, he said, "No, no, Mommy. I mean, where did I *come* from? Like Jimmy comes from Chicago."

She had not taken the time to clarify his *real* question.

We need to listen to *understand*. Paul Tournier, noted Swiss psychiatrist and author, says, "How beautiful, how grand and liberating this experience is, when people learn so to help each other. It is impossible to overemphasize the immense need men have to be really listened to. . . . Listen to all the conversations of our world, those between nations as well as those between couples. They are for the most part dialogues of the deaf."[1]

I tend to want to talk more than to listen. It is a habit which is quite ingrained, but God has been faithful to remind me of it. So it is exciting to see how He can root out an irritating habit if we ask Him, as long as we obey Him when He speaks to us about it.

I have found that memorizing Scripture is one of the best ways to have God speak to my heart. I've also learned the validity of the statement, "I used to memorize Scripture, but now I learn it *by heart*." In the past, I had sporadically memorized the Word of God for Sunday School contests and classes. But years ago when I started "learning it by heart" consistently and asking God to apply it to my everyday happenings, it changed my life.

It was after I had memorized Proverbs 18:2 that God started poking me quite frequently on the matter of listening to understand. Solomon said, "A fool does not delight in understanding, but only in revealing his own mind." When I would mentally be sitting on the edge of my chair just waiting for someone to finish so I could put my two cents worth in, God would remind me, "Carole, a fool does not delight in understanding, but only in revealing her own mind."

I'd say, "Ouch," then ask God to help me really listen to understand.

Interrupting another person is an infuriating habit and detrimental to listening. If we could stop this practice, part of the battle to listen intently would be won. But most of us interrupt continually and are totally unaware that we are doing it. Can this insidious habit be broken? Yes, if we would ask help from God and help from our mates. In private conversation (never, *never* in public, please), when our spouse interrupts, point it out. In love. Keep pointing it out to each other till the habit is broken. Pray together concerning an attitude of openness to allow for correction from the other partner. Ask for *God's power* to break the habit, for it must be broken.

An invaluable device to practice is to listen to the other person *without* interruption. Then the listener rephrases the speaker's statement. The speaker then has the opportunity to agree with or correct the listener's statement of what he or she said. Next, the listener becomes the speaker and the process is repeated.

Try it sometime. It takes discipline, but it can be a valuable tool in understanding and is especially helpful for times of conflict.

If communication is to occur, there must also be a listening to by the other person. Some may be thinking, *But my spouse doesn't interrupt; he never even listens!*

If this is the case, perhaps we need to do some self-examination to discover the reason why. Why aren't we being listened to? We may need to ask God to search our hearts and try our thoughts (see Psalm 139:23-24) to discover if there are bad habits, unkind words, and critical attitudes which are causing people not to listen to us.

A woman once told me, "My husband never listens to me. I could talk all day and he wouldn't hear a word I said!"

Well, *I* listened. It was a difficult task, but I did listen. For over an hour I listened to a woman who was hypercritical, sarcastic, and negative . . . and I felt sorry for that husband. She had built a climate of criticism into her marriage, and he had simply tuned her out. I had to admit that if I had been in his shoes, I'd have probably done the same thing.

God will help us be the kind of person worth listening to. The Bible says that the mouth of the righteous is a "well of life" (Proverbs 10:11, KJV). I sometimes wonder if mine is more like a babbling brook! Our creative God can and will give us truth worth sharing as we surrender to the Holy Spirit who gives us His fruit of love . . . and joy . . . and peace . . . and makes our mouths wells of life.

To listen and to be listened to is essential to communication. Only as we develop these traits will we really begin to understand each other and gain inroads into the mind and heart of the person whom God chose for us and of whom He said, "These two shall become *one*."

NOTES: 1. From *To Understand Each Other* by Paul Tournier, pages 29, 8. © 1967 by M. E. Bratcher. Used by permission of John Knox Press.

10

CHOOSING HONESTY
by Carole

HER FACE was puffy and red from weeping. Struggling for control, she said, "We were divorced a short time ago, but I still love him, and I'm sure he loves me. But we couldn't keep from fighting. A lot of it was my fault. I was constantly nagging him. . . ." She faltered, a sob blocking her efforts to continue.

They couldn't stop fighting.

That day, God gave her a fresh, new beginning as she invited Jesus Christ into her life to be her Saviour and Lord. And I know God will give her the strength and wisdom to stop the endless quarreling if she and her husband are reunited. I have every hope that they will "make it" the second time around.

Marriages are hurting if they are characterized by nagging, cutting sarcasm, and ridicule.

Ridicule devastates like a dum dum bullet, exploding the inner personality, destroying, tearing, and cutting great chunks of self away. A marriage characterized by derision, belittling, contempt, and the scorn of ridicule is grotesquely twisted and needs the hand of God to straighten it out.

Some necessary building blocks for marriage are

openness, sympathy, and understanding. Innermost thoughts should be freely expressed and uncritically received.

On some small back burner of my mind, an idea is always simmering. Most of these, when strained through Jack's objective collander, are without substance, but now and then I come up with a solid thought. If Jack ever ridiculed the worthless ideas, I'd have stopped verbalizing *all* of them long ago. But because of his understanding and acceptance, the creative concoctions of my mind simmer away happily.

His refusal to belittle even my wildest ideas has been a great help on our journey to intimacy in our marriage. His acceptance of my thinking processes has caused me to love him more deeply and it has helped me to be me. To be accepted unconditionally by another person is a totally freeing thing. One of the wonderful things about being a Christian is to know that God Himself accepts me totally and unconditionally when I come to Him through Christ. Jack has been an example to me of Christ's love in this way through the years.

Acceptance, openness, and understanding are vital ingredients to ask God to build into our lives. When people are ridiculed, they pull their heads into their shells and do not venture to stick them out again. Then they change, and the *real* person inside that outer covering may never be truly known. But to know and be known is essential to love and marriage.

So even though I am afraid to venture out of my shell, I *must* take the risk—and there is always risk—of exposing my tender skin to a possible verbal blade. I *have* to be vulnerable in a close relationship. At times, it will only be with the help of God and full trust in Him that I dare become vulnerable to possible hurt or rejection. But if I desire honest, open depth in that relationship, I must take that risk. Again and again and again.

The road to intimacy is blocked by ridicule. It is also obstructed by the wall of protective silence which we build around our feelings. The problem with building walls to keep hurt *out* is that the wall also isolates us *in*.

Sometimes building that wall is a totally unconscious thing. "Nothing is wrong" is a phrase that Jack and I have been trying to rid from our vocabulary. But it is hard. Especially for me.

When Jack does something which hurts or offends me, the first tactic to which I resort is silence. Being a rather loquacious person, Jack immediately senses something is wrong when I am quiet. Which is why I *am* quiet! If he didn't ask me about it, I would get worse. Knowing this, he is forced to ask, "Is there anything wrong?

My answer is, "No."

"Are you sure?" he will persist.

"Yes," I lie.

"Come on, Honey. I can tell something is bothering you. What is it?"

"Nothing," I respond. And on and on and on we go.

Basically, I guess, I don't tell him on the first go-round because I am either a bit ashamed at the silliness of the whole thing or I don't think Jack has suffered enough yet.

Childish? Yes.

Immature? Certainly.

Fair? Definitely not.

Whatever it is, I need to *get it out*. To say, "Yes, there is something wrong, but it is so inconsequential and silly that I am ashamed to tell you. I'd like the opportunity to get over it first."

Or, "Yes, but if I tell you right now, I'll cry, so please wait a few minutes."

Or even, "I'm not sure what's wrong. I think I really do feel like being quiet for a change. It has nothing to do with you."

A word of explanation is needed for love's sake. It will get your partner off the hook, or bring the problem out in the open. Either way, the loving, mature thing to do is to tear down the wall of silent hostility and expose it to God's cleansing light.

In my marriage to Jack, I am most guilty of using the "silent treatment." But it can also be the husband who retreats into silence. One of the most sorrowful cries I often hear from wives is, "My husband won't talk to me."

Cecil Osborne, counselor and former pastor, says:

> A woman's need for a close relationship is so great that if she cannot achieve it one way, she will instinctively try another. If her efforts at communication are balked by the husband's silence, she has all sorts of alternatives at her disposal: she may become angry over a trifle, or accusatory, or depressed. In an almost frantic attempt to force some kind of communication she will push any button on his control panel; if he finally erupts with anger, she will feel that she at least has gotten *some* response . . . . At a totally unconscious level the wife is saying, "I'd like first class love. If I cannot have that, I'll settle for attention. If I fail to get your attention, I'll get your sympathy. If that fails, I'll get you where it hurts—I'll have an accident or a symptom."[1]

I often wonder if men realize that when a wife picks a fight deliberately, it could be her way of saying she needs some attention, some response. But all too often silence is used by some men and women as a thrusting tool to frustrate and punish.

May God enable us to be mature, to handle our feelings in a responsible, adult way, to be open and understanding, and never, never use silence as a weapon to hurt.

NOTES: 1. From *The Art of Understanding Your Mate* by Cecil Osborne, page 53. Copyright © 1970 by Zondervan Publishing House, Grand Rapids, Michigan. Used by permission.

11

CHOOSING CONSTRUCTIVE CONFLICT
by Carole

A VALUE tag is attached to depth in communication: it is definitely worth the cost! The price is exacted in *time* (with the TV set turned off, getting up a bit earlier in the morning, a little less sleep at night when something needs to be discussed at length) and in *vulnerability*.

Many couples discover a tension-filled topic in their first year of marriage and bury it hastily for fear of creating problems. The second year another major issue surfaces, so they dig a grave for that one too. By year five, they are simply not talking about anything except surface issues. The silence screams, "Something is wrong," and all those buried conflicts grow increasingly rotten till the stench cannot be tolerated. Something is dead . . . and it could be the marriage.

Silence in a marriage may denote fear, a lack of caring what the other partner thinks, or an unwillingness to pay the price of deep sharing.

But silence isn't the only wall we have to overcome. Elmer and Sue set up a number of unconscious communication hurdles which caused them both to fall frequently in the dust.

1. *Too Busy*—One evening Sue said, "Elmer, I'd like

to talk with you about something that has been bothering me lately."

Elmer responded, "Not now, Sue. There's a football game on TV and I want to watch it. Let's talk about it later."

But somehow after dinner he had business that had to be taken care of and an important telephone call to make. After that he was just too tired. He had effectively blocked all real communication by being "too busy."

2. *Changing the Subject*—Two weeks later Elmer came home discouraged and upset. He had been wrestling with some personnel problems at work and wanted to talk about them with his wife. Just as he got the conversation started, Sue interrupted, "Honey, did you remember to pay the water bill yesterday?"

She had effectively indicated to him that she was not interested in his problems at work. (Later she complained that he never discussed his job with her.)

3. *Defensiveness*—So Elmer carried his problems alone. But the personnel problems did not dissolve and he became irritable. One night he tried to reach Sue again and said, "Sue, you don't seem very interested in my problems at work."

In quick succession, she looked stricken, hurt, and finally angry. She exploded, "You don't think so? Well, you don't listen to me either! How many times have I tried to tell you something and you kept right on reading your paper? Don't talk to me about not listening."

Defensiveness blocks necessary communication, yet we all practice it so successfully. It is the opposite of the biblical injunction to "walk in love and wisdom" (see Ephesians 5:2, 15).

Sue needed God's grace to respond with, "You're right, Elmer. I'm sorry. Tell me what I can do and how I can help you. I really will try to be a better listener and I am interested in your problems. Please forgive me." But she didn't do it.

4. *Super Guilt*—Sue's defensiveness caused Elmer to drop the subject and grow more silent and depressed. A week later Sue said, "Elmer, you have spent only 15 minutes with the kids this week, and even less with me. I really feel the need for more of your time."

Elmer responded, "You are absolutely right. I am the world's worst father and husband. I don't know how you put up with me. I am a total failure."

What could Sue say? He really wasn't *that* bad. So she reassured him and dropped the subject. Elmer had effectively blocked any in-depth talking by his expression of super-guilt. Dr. James Mallory of the Atlanta Christian Counseling Center has suggested that those who act or feel *this* guilty have no intention of changing, because if they did, they would not need to feel so guilty.[1]

4a. *Peace at Any Price*—A variation of the super-guilt attitude is the "peace at any price" giving-in person. Some husbands have abdicated their leadership in the family and gone down to defeat by this method. Content with exercising control at their office or job, their constant response at home is, "Do whatever you want to. You decide." This tactic makes the wife feel alone and insecure. Eventually this attitude leads to such repressed feelings of frustration in both husband and wife that joy is gone from their relationship and their communion is crushed.

5. *Rejection of Feelings*—Two days later Elmer said to Sue, "You know, I really am feeling like a failure in my work and as a husband and father. I feel very ineffective in my life right now."

He was finally being honest and vulnerable. But Sue

responded, "Oh, you shouldn't feel that way. It's dumb for you to feel that way."

The major problem was that Elmer *did* feel exactly that way. And all Sue's protests would not change the way he felt. Dr. Mallory writes:

> This disallowance of feeling, just because you don't happen to agree, is a very common block in communication. When you shoot back, "It's dumb to feel that way," or "How can you feel that way?" you are in fact hitting at the very core of the person. It represents a denunciation or belittlement. Rightly or wrongly the person has those feelings. They are part of him. Disallowing feelings is a deep rejection of the person himself. Instead, we should try to understand the person's feelings. This encourages communication and assists us to be helpful.[2]

Sue rejected Elmer's feelings about himself because they threatened her security in his job and in their relationship. But her rejection made him pull back further into his silence, trying to handle his frustrations by himself. His inadequacies had actually been reinforced by Sue's response.

Jack and I are learning that we must get things out in the open—to be real with each other, to share feelings and needs and desires. There are times, of course, when the best course is to end a discussion temporarily. Sometimes I have to quit because tears make it impossible for me to say more. At other times the edge of my anger is too sharp to risk saying anything because I know I may get destructive. But we must never withdraw permanently. We must come back to the issue at hand and resolve it or there will be untold consequences. But how in the world should we handle anger?

In a book I read, the author said that if you can handle anger positively by giving several positive statements to one negative statement, you should "give yourself a kiss." If you blew up and spouted out all your anger with venom and hostility, you should still "give yourself a kiss" because you have expressed your anger verbally rather than expressing it in other hostile ways which would have been more destructive.

It may be true that to express anger verbally is better than having an ulcer, or becoming frigid, dejected, or depressed. But instead of ventilating all the time, we need to turn to the Word of God. The Lord has a far better way for us to handle anger.

In studying God's ways of handling conflicts, Jack and I find these principles helpful for married couples to "have a really *good* fight," that is, to have a creative conflict under God's rules.

1. *Keep Cool!*—The Bible says that "a quick-tempered man acts foolishly" (Proverbs 14:17), and "a hot-tempered man stirs up strife, but the slow to anger pacifies contention" (15:18). God's Word further states that a man with a "cool spirit" is one with understanding (17:27-28). *That's* the kind of understanding we need.

Many factors help us in staying cool. Practicing *thinking* before we speak and learning to handle conflicts lovingly and without rancor are two of the most important. "The heart of the righteous ponders how to answer" (15:28), Solomon said, and "where there are many words, transgression is unavoidable. But he who restrains his lips is wise" (10:19).

In order to stay cool and not get angry or overly emotional, we may need to back away from the conflict for a time. "The beginning of strife is like letting out water, so abandon the quarrel before it breaks out" (17:14). This does not mean abandoning the *conflict* or working through to a solution, but when it becomes angry quarreling (or just before), leave it for a while. Come back to it after praying and thinking about it.

2. *Make Understanding Your Aim*—The aim in many of our conflicts seems to be to vent our anger and feelings at the other person. Solomon says, "A fool does not delight in understanding, but only in revealing his own mind" (18:2). In order to understand, we have to *listen* and hear the other person completely ("He who gives an answer before he hears, it is folly and shame to him"—18:13) and *try to see* the issue from the other's point of view.

So often we *presume* we know the facts and feelings of the other person. Yet "through *presumption* comes nothing but strife" (13:10). A conflict cannot be entered with the idea that one must "win." There is no winning or losing in a *good* conflict, but a breaking through to better understanding of each other. Otherwise you have both lost. When one person in a marital relationship is determined to win, *both* really lose because they have lost understanding and unity.

3. *Keep Short Accounts*—The Bible says that we are not to let the sun go down on our anger (Ephesians 4:26). This means that the deadline for solving a problem of anger and breaking through to a better understanding is the last time we see that person *that* day. For husbands and wives that would be bedtime; for conflicts at work sunset would be quitting time.

4. *Act Wisely, not Foolishly*—God says it is a foolish man who either gets angry or makes light of the other person's feelings or point of view. "When a wise man has a controversy with a foolish man, the foolish man either rages or laughs, and there is no rest" (29:9). Sol-

omon also says, "A fool always loses his temper, but a wise man holds it back" (29:11).

A wise person will not block the flow of God through his or her life with big chunks of self. God needs to control us in times of conflict as much as in times of calm. For His control at all times in our lives, we must practice Solomon's words of advice, "Do not let kindness and truth leave you; bind them around your neck, write them on the tablet of your heart. So you will find favor and good repute in the sight of God and man. Trust in the Lord with all your heart, and do not lean on your own understanding. In all your ways acknowledge Him, and He will make your paths straight" (3:3-6).

The following are ways in which you can do so: (1) be kind, truthful, and trusting that God will lead you; (2) do not be wise in your own eyes; (3) ask God to make you a wise person and remember that a wise person accepts correction (see 9:8); and (4) be aware of the tone of your voice. Try lowering it instead of raising it by remembering that "a gentle answer turns away wrath, but a harsh word stirs up anger" (15:1).

In handling their conflicts, Elmer and Sue have some learning to do and so do we. Being too busy to talk, half listening, defensiveness, and the disallowing of the other's feelings—all these must be considered. We must take a stand for open and free discussion, allowing feeling to be freely expressed. Depth, sharing, and openness can be fully experienced as we grow in our knowledge of God and of one another.

NOTES: 1. James D. Mallory, Jr., *The Kink and I* (Wheaton, Illinois: Victor Books, 1973), page 22.
2. *The Kink and I*, page 19.

12

CHOOSING TO BE OPEN
by Carole

WE WERE just finishing the breakfast dishes when Jack walked into the kitchen. "Where are my keys?" he asked hurriedly.

"In the top drawer," I responded.

"Those are *your* keys," he argued.

"No, they are yours," I countered emphatically. I had just had a new set made, so I was *positive* about whose keys were in that drawer. Convinced, he took them, thanked me, and walked out.

The young wife helping me with the dishes that morning had been visiting us for a few days. She turned to me with a thoughtful expression on her face and said, "Carole, I wish you would pray for me."

"I'd be happy to pray for you," I replied. "But how do you want me to pray?"

She answered sadly, "When my husband asks me a question the way Jack just asked you, he sounds angry."

"Oh?" I murmured. "Well, does he just *sound* angry or *is* he angry?"

After a moment's hesitation, she said sorrowfully, "I don't know."

"I don't know." These words echoed a hollow refrain

in my mind. I shook my head in wonder. We knew this couple well. Her concerns about her husband's state of mind were not new. Yet when he would ask her about something and sound angry, her questions were left unasked. Constantly his tone of voice had shouted to her that he was angry with her.

This situation points up the vital truth that we *must* learn to communicate when we are hurt . . . or frustrated . . . or angry.

This wife had never asked her husband the simple question, "Are you angry?" Instead she had assumed his anger, and her assumption was that he was angry with her. She felt insecure and unhappy—two feelings that had been growing within her for *years*.

All she needed was to ask her husband, "Are you angry?" This question would have communicated that he sounded angry to her and, if he wasn't, perhaps he needed to do something about the tone of his voice. If he really was angry and answered yes to her question, she undoubtedly would then have needed to ask, "Are you angry at me?" It just could have been that he had accidentally stubbed his toe in the bathroom and was mad at himself.

This couple needed to get their feelings out of all the musty closets of their lives and spring clean their marital house. Most of our difficulties come from misunderstanding one another because we won't *talk* and bring all those moldy things out into the open air. Instead, we seem to be content to read into one another's words, tone of voice, or silence, and we usually are very poor readers. A simple, clarifying question would save us hours, weeks, and even years of heartache and misunderstanding. Conflicts come because we haven't found out what the other person *means*.

Counselors generally agree that there are five levels in communication. John Powell, well-known writer on interpersonal relationships, words them as follows:

Level 5—Cliche conversation
Level 4—Reporting the facts about others
Level 3—My ideas and judgments
Level 2—My feelings (emotions)
Level 1—Peak communication[1]

Real communication begins at level three—my ideas and judgments. It is at this point that a person is willing to step out of his self-imposed solitary confinement and take a risk by telling a personal idea or thought to another person. He may still be cautious and, if he senses that what he is saying is not being accepted or listened to, he will retreat. If I tell you about an idea I have and you say, "That's dumb," it will be the last time I will share an idea with you. I have taken a risk and have been rejected. I will not risk again.

Level three then leads into and develops into levels two and one. Peak communication is when there is consistent and total empathy and understanding between two people.

In an everyday situation, the depth of levels in communication may work something like this:

The husband walks in the front door after work and his wife says, "Hi! How was your day?" This is level five —cliche conversation.

The husband answers, "Oh, OK." For some couples their big conversation of the day has just occurred.

But this wife wants to dialog, so she asks, "How did the meeting go this afternoon?"

Her husband responds, "Fair." Now we are at level four—reporting the facts. However, the question was a poor one. We have a "family joke" in our household about questions that can be answered with one word, because if they *can* be, they *will* be. A better question would have been, "What was the most important thing you discussed at your meeting?" or, "What was the attitude of the president toward your plan?"

The wife may now try to get to the feeling level (level two) by asking, "How did you *feel* the meeting went this afternoon?" only to have the husband respond on the third level with an idea or judgment. He may respond, "In my opinion, the committee came up with the wrong answers."

So she tries again, "Was that frustrating to you?"

"Yes," the husband declares. "I really felt badly that they hadn't done a better job of thinking through."

Now the couple is at a feeling level—the point of real communication . . . of talking of needs, disappointments, hopes, dreams. They may break through at any moment to level one—the open, total sharing with all defenses down.

That level might be reached when the man says, "I'm feeling so discouraged right now at my inability to help those men think through on the subject thoroughly. They aren't a team at all and somehow that has to be my fault. I seem to be inadequate for the job." And his wife accepts that empathetically, does not criticize his feeling that way, and begins working with him to overcome what he thinks are his inadequacies.

David Augsburger has said:

Communication is the meeting of meaning.

When your meaning meets my meaning across the bridge of words, tones, acts, and deeds, when understanding occurs, then we know that we have communicated . . . .

When two persons can share from the very center of their

existence, they experience love in its truest quality. Marriage is a venture into intimacy, and intimacy is the opening of one self to another.[2]

The Apostle Paul sums up our goal which is not to be immature children, but "to speak the truth in love" and *to grow up* into Christ (Ephesians 4:15). If all our conversations could be judged by that one phrase—"to speak the truth in love"—we would have both total and complete honesty and the kind of sensitive love we need to hear the real questions our wives or husbands are asking.

Being "totally transparent" and "speaking the truth in love" are quite different. Some people advocate the kind of transparency where we say everything that pops into our heads. Some feel we can't even know our own feelings unless we share them aloud with others. I disagree. Thoughts that are unkind and unloving, and attitudes that would burden the person to whom they might be ventilated, are best shared with God alone.

This is not to infer that we cannot share negatives. We can and we must. But negatives must *also* be shared in love. It is not loving to share things that cannot be changed. It might be true that I don't especially care for your big nose, but it is not kind or loving to tell you so. We must accept and overlook things that cannot be changed. Solomon put it this way, "Never forget to be truthful and *kind*. Hold these virtues tightly. Write them deep within your heart" (Proverbs 3:3, LB).

It is amazing what real love can accomplish in our lives.

I have a favorite story I love to tell. I never get bored hearing myself tell it even though I've told it hundreds of times. I enjoy the reactions of the listeners each time.

My husband has a favorite story that I have heard him tell dozens of times. Each time he tells it I enjoy hearing it again because in watching him get all wrapped up and engrossed in the events of the incident, he relives it and, vicariously, I relive it with him. We are one.

An acquaintance of mine has a favorite story she has told me at least five times. During the last four tellings I was bored to death.

What made the difference? The answer is found in Scripture: "Above all things have fervent love among yourselves; for love shall cover the multitude of sins" (1 Peter 4:8, KJV).

Most of us have a healthy self-love and this is right. It is the reason I don't get bored with my own storytelling. I deeply love my husband and don't get frustrated with his storytelling either.

But my acquaintance? Obviously my love lacks something when it comes to *her* favorite story. As I said, it is amazing what real love will accomplish.

This leads us to a question. If I get bored with someone who tells a story over and over, is that my problem or hers? Many times transparency (or telling a person that her story bores me to death—which is honest but not kind) is only our excuse to verbalize our own bad attitudes. It is our *attitudes* that need prayer; they need to be changed by God. The verbalizing of our bad attitudes only hurts the other person, and that is not loving.

Both "speaking the truth" and "in love" have to be considered. Those two statements need to be married forever and ever in our speech.

Keith Miller, one of the founders and leaders in the faith at work movement, has an excellent example of the difference between being honest and being transparent. He writes:

Several years ago when I was a new Christian, I decided I would try to be absolutely honest with my wife. We had just moved to a new town and had a good many extra expenses. This transition was making us a little nervous and frantic around the house. In the midst of everything Mary Allen went out and bought a new dress on sale, which she could not return. Buying something new sometimes has a soothing effect on her nerves, and understanding this, I was not too surprised or upset. So when she tried the dress on and asked me how I liked it, I told her I had seen a girl on First Street wearing one just like it that same day. First Street is a very unsavory part of the city. I said the dress was okay, but seeing a cheap-looking girl in one just like it spoiled it for me . . . which was all true. She just glared at me and *never wore the dress.* I was furious. We could not afford it anyway, but to buy the dress and *not wear* it was really terrible.

But I learned something that day. Christian honesty does not mean that I am obligated to express every thought that passes through my mind. I must learn to hear the *real* question someone is asking and answer *that* question, not just the one phrased by the outward words. This was the amazing genius of Jesus' conversation with people. He always saw through their superficial conversation to the real questions they were asking and dealt with them. Mary Allen had been wanting to know at a deep level, "Am I attractive to you? Is it all right that I impulsively bought this dress just because I feel frantic and dowdy right now? . . . Do you love me?" These were the real "woman questions"; and the true answer to all of them was "yes." But because of my insensitivity, I had answered the superficial question correctly with legalistic honesty—but by so doing, I had said "no" to her real questions.[3]

The adventure of marriage is exciting. We will never

get to know the person we are living with totally, but what a challenge to try. We are constantly changing and new vistas are always ahead.

My person is not a little hard core inside of me, a little fully-formed statue that is real and authentic, permanent and fixed; person rather implies a dynamic process. In other words, if you knew me yesterday, please do not think that it is the same person that you are meeting today.

I have experienced more of life. I have encountered new depths in those I love, I have suffered and prayed, and I am different. . . . Approach me, then, with a sense of wonder, study my face and hands and voice for signs of change; for it is certain that I have changed.[4]

NOTES: 1. John Powell, *why am i afraid to tell you who i am?* (Niles, Illinois: Argus Communications, 1969), pages 50-62.
2. David W. Augsburger, *Cherishable: Love and Marriage* (Scottsdale, Pennsylvania: Herald Press, 1971), pages 54-55.
3. Keith Miller, *Habitation of Dragons* (Waco, Texas: Word, Inc., 1970), pages 77-78.
4. *why am i afraid to tell you who i am?*, page 9.

13

CHOOSING THE HIGHEST
by Jack

THE YEAR before Carole and I were married, we
were separated by 300 miles. Both of us were busy.
In my last year of college, beside my studies, I was a
class officer and involved in athletics. Carole was
working 12 to 14 hours a day as a Christian Education Director. We had agreed that we would write to
each other every day. And we kept that agreement.

So every day I would go to my post office box on the
college campus, look in, and sure enough, there would
be a letter from Carole (and two on Monday).

Well, I found that I was so busy running about the
campus that I didn't have time to read her letters each
day. So I worked out a little scheme. I would save two or
two-and-a-half hours every Sunday afternoon for letter
reading time. On Monday, I would go to the post office,
get her letters, smell them, and then run off to class. That
night I would put her letters on my desk and concentrate
on my studies. On Tuesday, Wednesday, Thursday,
Friday, and Saturday I'd stack up those letters in the
order in which they arrived. Then on Sunday afternoon I
would look forward to sitting down, slitting each one
open very carefully, and reading them all through, pon-

dering over them till the time would be up and I'd have to get going again.

After we were married, we found ourselves still on a very busy schedule. While at seminary, we lived in a 27-foot by 8-foot trailer with a concrete path (to the bath, that is). Carole worked to help me through school, and beside studying I worked part time. We found it difficult to coordinate our schedules in such a way that we could stay in touch on a daily basis with everything we wanted to talk about. So we started carrying little notebooks around and from time to time as something came to mind that we wanted to be sure and tell the other, we would jot it down. On Sunday afternoons, we set aside a couple of hours to sit down with our notebooks, and communicate with one another to get caught up on all the things that had happened during the week.

Do you believe me? That isn't what happened at all! We *were* separated and we *did* agree to write one another every day. But when I went to the mailbox and found that letter, I would rip it open very unceremoniously. I would pull it out, stand right there in the middle of all the mooing herd in the post office area, and I was *alone* with Carole for the few minutes it took to read her letter. Then if my next class happened to be a particularly dull one, I would read her letter again even if it meant getting caught by the professor. When I got home in the evening, I would take a little time to read the letter more carefully, reading between the lines to try to figure out what she was really trying to say. We were in love with each other, and this was a love letter from her.

When we were married, we didn't carry little notebooks around to keep track of things. We stayed in touch with one another on a personal basis, and communicated with each other daily.

I use that illustration to point out that there are many Christians in the world who take a strange kind of approach to communicating with God. Their time with Him is relegated to a few minutes each week, perhaps only on Sunday. They set a little time aside on that day, which is the only time they devote to developing communication with God. God has given us the Bible in order to communicate great truths to us, truths He wants us to know regarding Himself, the world, man, and His Son Jesus Christ. But even more than that, He has given us the Bible to tell us things of a personal nature, to get inside our lives and deal with us on specific issues. Many Christians never take enough time to give God an opportunity to speak to them.

Perhaps some of you reading this book consider yourselves to be Christians, those belonging to Christ, those who have invited Jesus Christ to come into their lives to be their Saviour. Yet you have never taken the time over a period of months or years to get to *know* Him. Christ is living in you, He hears your every conversation, He penetrates your thought patterns, and He knows exactly what is going on inside your mind.

We need to get acquainted with Him and let Him talk to us through His Word. An occasional sermon or a Sunday School lesson once a week, while helpful, is not enough. These are like pre-digested food . . . someone else has gotten the "meat" from the Word of God, chewed it up, savored it, gotten nourishment from it, and then passed it on to us. It can help us, certainly, but such "milk" or "ground up" food is for babies. Growing children and mature adults need solid food, and even babies need to be fed more than once a week. In fact, babies need more feedings per day than adults because they can't take as much in at one time.

So God wants all of us, whether we are newly born into His kingdom or have been Christians for some time, to begin feeding individually and daily on His Word.

God, our heavenly Father, desires fellowship with us daily because He loves us. He has written us a love letter that He wants us to read so we can get to know Him. He has made available to us this beautiful thing we call prayer, which is our communication link with Him to let Him know what is on our hearts and to talk over with Him our problems, concerns, and things that are bothering us. We share with Him things that are causing us to be joyful and happy and that we are thankful for. We have an open channel of communication to Him in prayer and through the Bible.

Many people lose out on really *knowing* God because their approach to communicating with Him is like my hypothetical story. We read His love letter once a week (perhaps have it read to us in church), and we talk to Him when we get into a jam. But we fail to take advantage of the open access we have to fellowship with Him *on a daily basis.*

The Lord has said, "To this man will I look, even to him that is poor and of a contrite spirit, and trembleth at My Word" (Isaiah 66:2, KJV). *Trembles* here does not have the sense of being fearful, but trembling in the sense of being respectful and eager to find out what God has to say.

God's statement to Jeremiah has often challenged me:

> Let not the wise man glory in his wisdom, neither let the mighty man glory in his might. Let not the rich man glory in his riches, but let him that glorieth glory in this, that he understandeth and *knoweth Me,* that I am the Lord which exercise lovingkindness, judgment, and righteousness, in

the earth. For in these things I delight (Jeremiah 9:23-24, KJV).

God says that if you want to boast about something, it should not be because you are smart or powerful or strong or rich. It should be in the fact that you *know Him* in an intimate way because God delights in your knowing Him.

The psalmist makes quite a promise when he says, "Great peace have they which love Thy law and nothing shall offend them" (Psalm 119:165, KJV). What a motivation to get into the Word of God and find out what God wants to say to us. Our approach to the Bible should be like listening to a *voice* rather than reading a book. We should hear His voice saying, "This is your Father speaking. Listen!" If He has taken the trouble to put into writing the thoughts, ideas, and words He wants to communicate to us, He wants to be listened to and obeyed. When God speaks, He means to be taken seriously.

It takes three people to make a lasting marriage—a man, a woman, and God. Our communication link to each other as husband and wife has to be forged stronger as the years go by. Even more vital is our communication link individually with the One who created us both.

How much time can you give out of 24 hours to talk with God? You need eight hours for sleep and eight for work, then perhaps two to eat. That leaves about six. What can you give God out of your free six hours each day?

Some can give Him an hour, some 30 minutes, some 15. If you have never developed a time to spend each day with God, don't start with any of those larger amounts of time. Try just seven minutes a day to spend all alone in

God's presence. Here is how to spend that precious
seven minutes.

1. *Half a minute—Pray.*

In that 30 seconds, pray, "Open Thou mine eyes, that I
may behold wondrous things out of Thy law" (Psalm
119:18, KJV). You might say something like, "Now,
Lord, I am going to open Your Word in just a minute to
read it and see what You have to say to me. I pray that
You will open the eyes of my spiritual understanding
that I might be able to grasp what it is that You are trying
to say to me personally today."

2. *Four minutes—Read God's Word.*

If this is new to you, start with the Book of Philippians, which is a warm and intimate book the Apostle
Paul wrote to Christian friends. Don't try to read a whole
chapter. Take a few verses and read them slowly and
thoughtfully. Think about them, and ask, "What is God
saying to me from them?"

3. *Two-and-a-half minutes—Pray.*

It may be that God has said something to you which
you need to pray over. You may need strength and help
to *do* what He has told you to do. Spend a moment
thanking Him and praising Him for being so good to
you. Tell Him of the burdens and problems that are
uppermost in your mind. Pray through your day,
appointments, situations, meetings, and problems you
might be facing.[1]

In order to do this effectively, you are obviously going
to need to find a time and a place. If we are going to
fellowship with God, we need to give Him the *best* part
of the day. He deserves that. The time will be different
for various individuals. For some, the best part of the
day is in the morning. Some "night people" will be most
alert in the evening. For a busy mother, it might be the

children's naptime; for a businessman, lunch time could be best.

But find a time when it is quiet for your time alone with God.

If you will do this consistently for four weeks, I will give you an iron-clad guarantee. I will guarantee you that you will begin noticing a difference in your own life. Changes of attitude will begin to take place; you will become more sensitive to sin in your life.

Next, your mate will begin to notice these changes. You will be a nicer person with whom to live, a more enjoyable individual to be around, because God will begin to change things in your life that will make a difference in your marriage relationship.

Paul states categorically that "all Scripture is given by inspiration of God, and is profitable for doctrine, for reproof, for correction, for instruction in righteousness" (2 Timothy 3:16, KJV).

• For doctrine—so that we might know the great truths that are revealed in the Word of God.

• For reproof—so that we might hear God's rebukes and reprimands concerning our sins and manner of life.

• For correction—so that we might change and rectify our behaviour when He has reproved us.

• For instruction in righteousness—so that we might live the kind of life that reflects Jesus Christ consistently.

Paul then gives us the reason: "That the man [or woman] of God may be adequate [or perfect, mature, growing toward maturity], equipped for every good work" (3:17). That is fantastic. God does not say we have to have a college degree, go to a certain kind of church, or have unique gifts and abilities. He says that if we are faithful to get into the Word, it will be profitable in four ways and the result of that will be Christian maturity.

And His Word will equip us to serve God in whatever way He wants us to serve Him.

Take me up on my guarantee today, for "today is the first day of the rest of your life!" Use it to communicate with God and strengthen your marriage.

NOTES: 1. A longer explanation of this quiet time with God may be found in the pamphlet by Robert D. Foster, *Seven Minutes with God*, obtainable from your local Christian bookstore.

14

CHOOSING SOME "NEVERS"
by Jack

CAROLE and I were sitting in a motel dining room having breakfast when we became aware of a conversation near us. A couple was discussing finances and the man had just told his wife of some investment plans he was considering.

Suddenly the woman's strident voice rose above the noise of the diners as she exclaimed, "And where do you think you are going to get that kind of money? What are you going to do, sell my underwear?"

All eyes turned toward the pair. The man flushed, looked down, and never spoke a word.

It was the ultimate sarcastic remark—a cut-down that was a perfect put-down. Obviously, she had grown quite adept with her verbal rapier.

Momentarily I wondered if Carole and I could have ever grown so proficient. I thank God that He detoured us from that muddy road years ago.

Some things Carole and I simply never do. I often refer to these as the "nevers" in our relationship, because we have learned that for a couple they spell disaster.

The number one never for us is: *never use sarcasm in conversing with one another.*

The dictionary defines *sarcasm* as, "A sharp and often satirical or ironic utterance designed to cut or give pain . . . a mode of satirical wit depending for its effect on bitter, caustic, and often ironic language that is usually directed against an individual." It comes from a Greek word meaning "to tear flesh, bite the lips in rage, sneer."[1] A perfect illustration is the woman's remark concerning the selling of her underwear.

In our American culture, we have become adept at the sarcastic remark. Many of our TV situation comedies are based on it, such as, "All in the Family" and "Maude." Don Rickles has made a fortune from it. But in marital relationships it is a "never" for Carole and me.

This was not always true. Shortly after we were married, we discovered that we had developed an ingrained habit of the sarcastic joke in kidding one another. At first, as we made little barbs and sharp remarks, they were totally harmless. We meant nothing by them. But over a period of a couple of years, we began to discover that this habit had become a convenient way of getting in a good dig at the other partner every now and then. The other person did not know whether it was to be taken seriously or not. We could hint at a truth in our sarcasm that we were afraid to share honestly; and the other, not knowing if the intent was serious, was unable to take offense. We discovered that we were hurting one another.

One summer, about two years after we were married, we worked with a pastor and his wife and spent many hours with them. It was obvious to us that this older couple was deeply in love and had a great time together. Gradually we began to notice that in all the hours we spent with them, we never heard them resort to sarcasm as a means of joking or kidding one another. Halfway through the summer, we asked them about it. Interestingly, they related our own story back to us. They had also found themselves hurting each other by sarcasm after they were married and found it convenient to use a sharp barb when they didn't like something in the other partner. When they recognized what they were doing and the hurt it was causing, they prayed about it together and covenanted with each other to stop doing it. It took some time because it had become an unconscious habit, but finally they conquered it with the help of the Lord. They shared with us what a great difference it had made in their marital relationship.

Following their example, Carole and I did the same thing. We prayed about it, confessed it as sin, and covenanted with one another to drop it from our lives. It took a few weeks to even get to the place where we were conscious when we did it. It had become so ingrained in our speech that it was almost automatic to come back with a nasty crack. It was hard to remind each other about it, but finally we eliminated it from our kidding vocabulary.

Couples, even whole families, commonly make the ones they love the brunt of a put-down. Some are totally unaware of the shadow of hurt on the other's face as the barb finds its mark. As we entered a church where we were to have a weekend seminar on the marriage relationship, we met the pastor. As he was introduced to us, he quipped sarcastically, "Well, I'm sure going to pay my wife's way for this one!" He had become adept at the barb game.

A second never for us is: *never criticize or correct one another in public.*

A husband and wife are leaving a party, and he says to the host, "Thanks for inviting us over. It's such a welcome change from TV dinners." Funny? Maybe. Kind? No.

Or the husband says to the man who is giving him some directions, "You'd better tell me. Jeannie could get lost with a police escort." Funny? Maybe. Kind? No.[2] This sort of remark not only is unkind, but it makes one's mate look small. Do we *really* want our spouses to look small in the eyes of other people? We need to love more than that.

Many things we do cause others to look small in the eyes of friends. Sometimes a wife asks her husband to tell his favorite story at a gathering of friends. She has coaxed him, knows it is a favorite of his, and he loves to tell it. So he begins his story. He gets into it and leaves something out. So she says, "Oh, honey, you left out the part about . . . ," and he backs up and puts in that detail.

As he goes into another section of the story and changes a percentage, she corrects him. In another part he adds a statement that she has not heard before, so she sets him straight. (After all, it is *his* story; he should be able to tell it like he wants to, with any changes he pleases.)

After the fourth correction in front of his friends, he finally explodes, "Oh, *you* tell it!"

Why do we think it is our God-given right or responsibility to correct our mates anywhere, under any conditions, no matter what? It is a tragic habit with terrible consequences. It throws water on the fire of spontaneity and love.

I am the president of the Carole Mayhall Fan Club! Now she has some other fans, but I am the president. And the reason I am a fan of hers is not because she is such a fantastic cook or a wonderful mother or a godly woman or any other such reason. The reason that I am the president of the Carole Mayhall Fan Club is simply because *I love her*. And because I love her, I want her to look good in the eyes of other people.

A third never for us, more especially for me, is: *never drop a delayed bomb*.

What do I mean by "a delayed bomb"?

One night Carole and I were about to go out to dinner. We were reading in the living room a few minutes before leaving and she made no move to get ready. Totally unthinking, I said, "Aren't you going to change?" What a mistake! It was a mistake because *she already had changed*.

Being a sensitive woman, her next question was, "Why? Don't you like what I've got on?"

What could I say? I lamely responded, "Well, there are other dresses that you have that I like better."

That was a delayed bomb. The reason it was delayed—about two years anyhow—was that when she had bought that dress, I had told her I liked it. And the fact was that I never had.

I learned a hard truth that day. I knew the validity of the statement, "If you like it, say so." Now I was learning the *practicality* of the opposite truth, "If you don't like it, say so." Immediately, but *in love*—not two years later.

Carole couldn't help but wonder how many other dresses she had in her closet that I didn't like and hadn't told her about. I need to learn to "speak *the truth* in love," consistently, always, and forever, and without fail.

The "nevers" in our relationship can be summed up in one word—kindness. Sarcasm, criticism, and delayed bombs are simply not *kind*. And to love a person is to be kind to that person. It is to practice steadfastly God's admonition for us to be kind one to another (see Ephesians 4:32).

NOTES: 1. By permission. From *Webster's New Collegiate Dictionary*. © 1977 by G. & C. Merriam Co., Publishers of the Merriam-Webster Dictionaries, page 1025.
2. Adapted from Charlie Shedd, *Letters to Philip* (Garden City, New York: Doubleday & Company, Inc., 1968), page 60.

15

CHOOSING TO PAY THE PRICE
by Jack

HE WAS a very busy man; his wife felt that he was too busy. It had been some time since they had spent some private time together in his crowded schedule. So when she came across his appointment book one day, she wrote in her own name for "12:00 lunch on Tuesday" and didn't say a word to him.

A couple of days later she looked on his Tuesday calendar and found that her name had been neatly crossed out and a business appointment written in. Her husband hadn't said a word to her either.

The wife tells this story with a rueful smile. It's a wonder that she can still manage that.

We have a price to pay for depth in sharing in another's life. And the one payment that will yield the greatest interest is *time together*. And one of the most valuable means of keeping in touch with another's heart is to play "The Dating Game" regularly.

Carole and I started dating nearly three decades ago and we intend to keep on dating till we can't hobble out the door any longer. Our goal is to have a date once a week, though we don't always achieve our aim. To get away from the house, the phone, the mad jumble of things, and to get *alone* is the point. We may have a candlelight dinner at our favorite restaurant or just a McDonald's hamburger or a pizza. *Where* we go is relatively unimportant. *Going* is the major thing.

The purpose for going out on a date is to talk. We want to get caught up with one another's inner thoughts and heartbeat. We find in these times that we get into subjects that we don't think to talk about in our busy days at home when interruptions are frequent. Our kind of date doesn't need to cost much, or cost anything at all. A drive to a favorite park, a picnic, a bicycle ride on a spring day. In our graduate school days, when money was nonexistent, we would go to a large department store, seclude ourselves in a little private record booth, and play all the newest records. When we could really splurge, we would even *buy* a 45-rpm record for about 50¢.

Dates don't have to be costly, but the price must be paid in *discipline* and in *time*—the discipline of making it a priority, of saying no to some other projects, the discipline of *taking the time*.

Another thing Carole and I do is trade off with one another in planning dates. It's a lot of fun. The husband plans things he knows his wife enjoys (window shopping? picnics?), while the wife reciprocates (golfing? mountain climbing?). The idea of a date is to get time alone together. Our double dating stopped after college. I don't mean that we no longer go out with other couples, but that time doesn't count as *our date*. When the children are little and money is scarce, dating takes more doing. Trading off with the neighbors on the babysitting part may work; it will be well worth the trouble, and we feel it is a big factor in keeping the romance and sparkle in any relationship.

But once a week dating isn't enough. Another goal every couple should aim for is a few minutes *each day* to stay in touch.

Over the years, we have had to do this at different times because of our changing schedules and circumstances—our daughter growing up, people living in our home, changes in work responsibilities. Now that we are alone, we do it at breakfast. In the last several years, when we've had people living in our home, we'd wait till they had to leave for work and then sit down together. We would take 20 or 30 minutes to linger over a third cup of coffee and talk. Occasionally I have a breakfast meeting, but as much as possible we consider breakfast as *our time*. We guard it jealously because we need it to stay in touch with one another and to continue forging the links of our lives together.

For deep and growing communication, the price is paid in time. It takes time to enjoy one another on dates. It takes disciplined periods sectioned from our lives each day to explore our hearts fully. And it takes a multitude of fragments snatched from the minutes of each day that insure depth of meaning in our lives together.

16

CHOOSING TO OVERLOOK
by Jack

WE WERE running 15 minutes late and were rushing to get dressed for an important dinner when it
happened for the tenth time that week. Carole and I
arrived at our "closet-with-the-sliding-door" at precisely the same instant. For a second we stood staring at
each other. Then we burst into laughter, and I bowed in
exaggerated jest, motioning her to go ahead and get her
things out first. With a sliding door closet, only one part
can be opened at a time.

I had not always been able to laugh. I had gone
through occasions when my thoughts had grumbled
and then flared, "Why does she *always* have to get into
the closet when *I* need to?"

On such trivial matters, marriages hang together or
fall apart.

Carole and I have been in the school of learning daily
relationships ever since we met. We went together for
three-and-a-half years on the same college campus and
the pressure this caused was acute. I am a perfectionist
and over the months a number of Carole's habits and
mannerisms began to irk me. Simultaneously, little
things I would say or do bothered her. These things

piled up over a period of weeks till one final item would
start the "can you top this?" game of irritation sharing.
Two or three days would be spent in resolving our
problems.

When this had happened several times, we realized
we had a problem which we could not handle, and
decided to ask the advice of Dr. Brooks, a godly dean at
our college. He listened to our story, smiled knowingly,
and gave us some of the best advice we've ever had. He
said, "Mrs. Brooks and I have been married over 30
years. If we had let the little things that irritated us about
one another *build up,* we would probably have been
divorced years ago. But early in our marriage we learned
that we had to forgive and forget, to overlook and make
allowances for, and accept each other for what we were.
Some things needed to be talked about and solutions
found, but things that *couldn't be changed* must be forgiven immediately and forgotten."

That was so practical. So when a little thing began to
fester, we immediately exposed it, discussed it, and
decided together what could be changed. When I told
Carole that the bobby pins she wore in her hair poked
me in the cheek when she put her head on my shoulder,
she changed her hairstyle and has never worn bobby
pins since. No big deal. And she helped me correct
sentences in which I was using incorrect grammar.

But the things that couldn't be changed, such as the
inability to play golf well, to think with complete logic,
to feel intuitively when one is depressed, to tell a joke so
that the punch line comes out right, we asked God for
the ability to forgive, forget, and accept about each
other.

In the early years together, irritations can literally
bombard a couple. Men who leave socks in the middle of

the bedroom, don't hang up their pajamas, and leave globs of toothpaste in the bathroom marry neat, precise women who snatch a newspaper away before the husband is finished reading it to put it away in its proper place.

We've certainly had our share. I have to laugh in retrospect at all the lessons we learned through that one "closet-with-the-sliding-door." At times when we *didn't* arrive at the closet at the same moment, I would try to open my side, only to have the door stop short. Looking in on Carole's side, I would see a nice neat row of three pairs of shoes that weren't *quite* in the closet. That would irk me to no end. I would think, *Why in the world can't Carole put her shoes all the way into the closet?* So I would *kick* them in.

Sometimes I would reach into the shower stall to turn on the water and instead of a nice, bright, shiny cold faucet I would touch a soggy washcloth draped over the faucet. What a terrible way to begin a shower!

These irritations need to be talked about. Those that cannot be changed, such as arriving at the closet door simultaneously, need to be treated with humor, forgiven, and forgotten.

One thing I *still* cannot figure out. How is it that I can take off two socks, dutifully put them in the dirty clothes hamper, have them go through the washing and drying process, and have only one sock get back into my drawer? We must have a washer that eats socks. Carole has even solved this irritation. She simply does not put one sock back anymore till the other one shows up. Of course I have to have a little larger inventory of socks that way!

These are all funny, stupid, frustrating, and trivial matters of our existence. Yet so many relationships are destroyed over them. But our God is in control over even the funny, stupid, frustrating, and trivial matters. He is not only in the business of changing people, but He can help us be creative in our solutions for changing the habits of our lives. He has helped me learn to hang up a bath towel with the monogram right side out and precisely centered. I don't leave my pajamas in the center of the bedroom any more (I pile them in a neat little stack by the wall now). Carole doesn't hang the washcloth over the shower faucet but on an added towel rack.

We are learning, with God's help, to adjust, to change, and to accept. And we have discovered that even that can be fun.

17

CHOOSING TO FOLLOW THE WAY
by Carole

AFTER an afternoon at the county fair, two country boys discovered they each had only a quarter left. One decided to ride the merry-go-round, but the other declined. When the first boy finished his ride, he asked his friend why he hadn't ridden with him. The second boy replied, "Well, you spent all your money, you got off where you got on, and you *ain't been nowhere*."

How many of us feel something of the same? We look back on some days and think, *We've spent all our money, we got off where we got on, and we ain't been nowhere.*

God would not have it so. He wants each of us to be *somebody*, to go *somewhere*, and to have a life that is full of meaning and purpose.

How is this possible?

We had lived in the Chicago area a number of years when a friend invited me to have lunch with her at the Deerpath Inn in a northern suburb. (Just how far north it was I was to discover later.) She had given me directions from my home in a northeastern suburb, but I started out from a location nearer to Lake Michigan. Somehow I had it fixed in my mind that Deerpath Inn was in Deerfield. My logic centered in the fact they both began with "deer." Actually, the restaurant is in Lake Bluff, a few suburbs north of Deerfield.

I thought I knew a quicker route to Deerfield than she had given me, so I started up a main diagonal road. I drove and drove and drove and couldn't find Illinois Road, where she had directed me to turn. By this time I was late and a bit frantic. So I did what women will do and men seem to have a hard time doing . . . I got off the road and went into a filling station to ask for some directions.

I looked at the attendant hopelessly and said, "Please, can you help me? I'm lost."

He asked, "Where are you going?"

"Deerpath Inn," I responded.

"Oh, OK," he replied and scratched his head. "Let's see, you go one block north and three blocks east . . . no, that's not so good. Go three blocks north and two blocks east . . . well, perhaps a better way is for you to go . . ."

He told me three different ways to go, and by this time I was utterly confused.

A nicely dressed gentleman was in the station at the time, standing there and taking it all in. Finally, he turned to me and said, "Would you like to follow me to your destination?"

I thought, *Whew! Would I!*

The attendant asked him if he was going to Deerpath Inn, and the man replied, "No, but I live in Lake Bluff and will be going right past it. I would be happy to show this lady the way."

So I said, "Thank you so much," and he got in his car and I in mine and we started out in an entirely different direction than the three ways the station attendant had suggested.

We drove on the tiniest, squiggliest, awfullest, backest roads you ever saw in your life. And you can imagine what was going through my mind all this time. *Where is he taking me? What is he going to do when he gets me there?* I was so horribly lost that I felt committed to wherever he was taking me.

It seemed like an eternity, but I'm sure it was just a few short minutes till we turned on to Illinois Road and pulled up in front of the Deerpath Inn. This man was even so kind as to get out of his car, come back to mine, and bend down to ask through my window, "Now do you think you can find your way back?"

I smiled, and assured him that my friend would help me.

I couldn't help thinking afterward that this experience was an interesting parallel to life.

Most of us start out on our journey of life fairly confident that we know where we are going and how we are going to get there. Of course in my generation the goal for many women was to "get married and live happily ever after" (a very short-range and unrealistic goal for sure). We think we have the necessary knowledge of direction and purpose in life.

And so we begin. We go till something makes us realize that we aren't getting anywhere. An empty marriage, a child that isn't turning out the way we hoped, an illness, a death, financial reverses . . . or maybe just a hollow feeling deep down inside that tells us there has to be more to life than we are experiencing. Something makes us realize that we are lost.

We begin by searching for the way to fulfillment, but we obtain confusing directions. One person tells us that a career will fulfill us. We may believe that till we read a quote such as I read in *Family Weekly* a short time ago by

Taylor Caldwell, well-known author. She was asked if putting her book *Captains and Kings* on a nine-hour TV production brought her the solid satisfaction that seemed denied her by Hollywood's failure to make any films of her previous books. Her answer was heartbreaking:

> There is no solid satisfaction in any career for a woman like myself. There is no home, no true freedom, no hope, no joy, no expectation for tomorrow, no contentment. I would rather cook a meal for a man and bring him his slippers and feel myself in the protection of his arms than have all the citations and awards and honors I have received worldwide, including the Ribbon of Legion of Honor and my property and my bank accounts. They mean nothing to me. And I am only one among the millions of sad women like myself.[1]

Another person tells us that our fulfillment comes in quality education. We listen to others telling us to immerse ourselves in our families in order to fulfill our lives. Some say enrichment comes through power or money. But as we try these methods and directions, nothing seems to fill that vacuum which keeps telling us we haven't yet found the answer.

At some point in our lives we are confronted with the One who looks at us tenderly and asks, "Would you like to follow Me?"

This Person looks as though He could be the Way . . . and someone else may have told you that He is, but each individual has to make the decision as to whether to believe Him and accept His credentials. I am speaking, of course, of Jesus Christ. He made some astounding claims. He claimed to be God . . . and He had to be in order to be the Way for us. He claimed to have the power to forgive sins, to give us not only eternal life in the future but a new quality of life here and now (John 10:10).

You see, we have not only lost the way to a fulfilling *life*, but the reason we don't have a fulfilling life is because we are lost to God Himself. We are lost . . . separated from God by our rebellion against Him, by insisting on going on our own way, and by all the things that are wrong with our lives. As a just and holy God, He has to judge these sins. God stands in front of me, as it were, and reads off all the things that are wrong with me, and the list is quite long. He would say to me, "Carole, you are a selfish, wilful, proud, jealous, and angry person," and on and on He could go. In all honesty I would have to admit, "Yes, Lord, You are absolutely right!" And God being God has to judge and exact payment.

But then Jesus Christ steps forward and says, "But remember, Father, I have already borne the penalty of all those sins Carole has committed. I came down to earth at Your command . . . lived a perfect life . . . and met all Your requirements for righteousness, so that there is no need for Carole to pay the consequences of sin which are death and separation from You. And I chose to give My life on the cross . . . and I did it for Carole and for all who have sinned." (See Romans 3:23 and 6:23.)

Then the Father says, "Of course, I remember." He now turns to me and asks, "What are you going to do about it? Do you accept the sacrifice of My Son?"

I have a choice to make. I can say, "Thank You, Lord, I accept Your sacrifice. Thank You for taking my penalty on Yourself by dying for me. I accept You as my Saviour and Lord." And at that moment I am cleansed from all my sins and become a child of God. I am born into the family of God and become a "Christ-one" or Christian.

Or I can say, "Thank You, but I'll try to do it my own way." If I respond this way, Christ looks sadly at me and says, "Carole, there is no other way. I am the Way, the Truth, and the Life. No one can come to the Father except through Me." (See John 14:6.)

If I reject His offer, I continue to be spiritually dead . . . lost to God and lost to being a fulfilled person.

Jesus Christ is our only way to life without end . . . to a dimension in our lives and relationships that will be rich with meaning and love. He is the source of love, of joy, of peace. When you have Him—when you say yes to His invitation to follow Him and ask Him to be your Saviour and Lord—never again will you feel that you have been on a merry-go-round heading nowhere.

NOTES: 1. Taylor Caldwell, "Ask Them Yourself," *Family Weekly*, September 19, 1976. Reprint by permission of FAMILY WEEKLY, copyright © 1976, 641 Lexington Avenue, New York, N.Y. 10022.

What Is Involved in Love

18

CHOOSING TO OBEY GOD
by Jack

IT WAS a nightmare and I wanted desperately to pinch myself awake. Only pinching didn't help because it was real.

I had been speaking at a conference outside a small village in The Netherlands. Having an afternoon to myself, I borrowed a car to go into town for some shopping. The "small village" turned out to be a thriving little city with streets going off in all directions. Apparently in turning off the main road, I had lost my sense of direction and found myself hopelessly lost.

It is one thing to be lost in a country where you know the language. It is another to be surrounded by people with whom you can't converse.

I was greatly relieved when I finally found a kind, English-speaking hotel clerk who offered to help me. But when I started to ask directions back to the conference grounds, I suddenly realized that I didn't know the name of the conference center, nor the road on which it was located. And everyone I knew in Holland who *might* know was already at the conference.

I stared at the clerk in consternation. What a predicament to be in! Finally, after quite some time of telephoning all possible conference facilities within a radius of 20 miles, my benefactor located the place from which I was lost.

At times, we are unaware of having lost our sense of direction. Later, however, there is a growing realization we are lost, when we can't discover any clues to familiar ground.

Many Christian husbands today are "lost" in an area of their marriages and don't even know it. When they discover they have been traveling a wrong road, they don't know where to begin to get "found" again.

Some men don't even care that they are heading in the wrong direction. Some are actually deluded into thinking that they are doing right and pleasing God, even while they are disobeying some of His commands.

The particular command, which some ignore, many do not understand, and most can't do, is given to us three times within a single paragraph by the Apostle Paul. It is the command to *love your wife* (Ephesians 5:25, 28, 33).

"Nonsense," you might respond. "I love my wife. I wouldn't have married her otherwise."

But *do* you? Do you love her in the way *God commands* you to love her?

We were in a home which is dedicated to serving Christ. All the family members give of themselves, their time, and their energies to bringing men and women to Jesus and to helping them grow into productive disciples. The husband in this household truly "denies himself"—in terms of time, energy, relaxation. But unconsciously perhaps, he may feel that because he and his wife are "one," it is alright for him to deny *her* his time, energy, and times for relaxation as well.

Paul wrote:

Husbands, *love your wives, just as Christ also loved the church* and gave Himself up for her; that He might sanctify her, having cleansed her by the washing of water with the Word, that He might present to Himself the church in all her glory, having no spot or wrinkle or any such thing; but that she should be holy and blameless. So husbands ought also to *love their own wives as their own bodies.* He who loves his own wife loves himself; for no one ever hated his own flesh, but nourishes and cherishes it, just as Christ also does the church, because we are members of His body. For this cause a man shall leave his father and mother, and shall cleave to his wife, and the two shall become one flesh. This mystery is great, but I am speaking with reference to Christ and the church. Nevertheless let each individual among you also *love his own wife even as himself;* and let the wife see to it that she respect her husband (Ephesians 5:25-33).

According to the Word of God, the husband is commanded to love his wife in an extraordinary manner. He is to love her in the same way that Christ loves the Church, as he does his own body, and as he loves himself. That is one tall order!

Throughout the New Testament, we as Christians are commanded to love one another. But this is the only place in all of the Bible where one person is commanded to love another *in the same way* as Christ loves the Church. God ordained this relationship to exist between a husband and a wife. It is uniquely different from any other in all of His creation.

Tragically, some men have a more unique relationship with their set of golf clubs. Or the ministry in which they are involved. Or even with their children. Somehow many wives come out as the lowest person on the totem pole.

John said, "Let us not love with word or with tongue, but in deed and truth" (1 John 3:18). A man who denies his wife his own self, his energy, his time, and his thought does not love his wife in deed (by his actions) nor in truth. Neither does he love her the way Christ loved the Church—which was and is totally giving of Himself.

Love and admiration are necessary both for a husband and wife. But to be loved is more important for a woman, while admiration is significant to a man.

It is important that a woman *know* she is loved. And that love has to be communicated in such a way that she *feels* it. Love has to be manifested in terms of words *and* actions.

The epitome of love is expressed best in what has been called the "Love Chapter" in the Bible. Notice the descriptive words that denote *action* in this passage:

> Love is very patient and kind, never jealous or envious, never boastful or proud, never haughty or selfish or rude. Love does not demand its own way. It is not irritable or touchy. It does not hold grudges and will hardly even notice when others do it wrong. It is never glad about injustice, but rejoices whenever truth wins out. If you love someone you will be loyal to him no matter what the cost. You will always believe in him, always expect the best of him, and always stand your ground in defending him (1 Corinthians 13:4-7, LB).

From time to time it would be a good idea for all of us who are married to read this passage together while holding hands, then make a fresh commitment in asking God for this kind of love for one another.

When God speaks, He means to be taken seriously.

When He tells husbands to love their wives, not once, but three times in one passage, it must be important to God that men do it. The major question, of course, is how?

In order to communicate to Carole that I love her, I try to do three things every single day. I don't always reach this goal, but I try.

The first is to tell *her that I love her.*

A cartoon showed a wife asking her husband over and over, "Do you love me?" He would not answer her till, in exasperation in the last frame, he shouted, "Of course I love you. That's my job!"

The man was certainly right. It *is* our job. But somehow I don't think his answer satisfied his wife.

One man got so tired of hearing his wife ask him if he loved her day after day that he went into his workshop and engraved a little wooden plaque with the words "I love you." He then took it to the kitchen, hung it over the sink, and brought his wife in to see it. "There," he said triumphantly, "I have said it! It's in writing! Now let's forget it!" I don't believe his answer satisfied his wife either.

That approach simply won't work. A wife needs to hear that she is loved and hear it often. It doesn't have to be a romantic setting all the time. A quick "I love you" as you walk out the door, another as she's cooking supper, or a small hug and a whisper as you pass each other in the hall will do wonders.

I aim every day to tell Carole that I love her.

My second goal is to do something nice for her each day.

This one is more difficult. It takes considerable creativity and thought. Dawson Trotman, founder of The Navigators, said many times, "Think—there is so little competition."

Many wives, subconsciously or consciously, think of their homes as an extension of their personalities, especially if the wife is not working outside the home. As she has more time to give to her home, the rooms begin to reflect the kind of person she is. Husbands would do well to remember that. When a husband neglects those little things around the home that she has asked him to do—in fact sometimes nagged him to do—she takes it personally. It speaks to her in terms of love. If she is thinking of her home as an extension of herself, then when her husband neglects *it*, he neglects *her*. Men rarely see it that way. Little jobs around the house are 20th down on their priority lists.

For you to demonstrate your love for your wife, you must try to see things from her point of view. What does your wife enjoy doing that doesn't take much effort but at the same time would please her? Carole enjoys windowshopping at an enclosed shopping center near our home. On the other hand, walking around on the hard cement and staring in glass windows is not exactly my idea of having a good time. Yet I know she enjoys it. And I enjoy being with her. So, on occasion, I try to get home a little early from work and suggest that we go and do some windowshopping. It takes a little time, a little energy, a little sacrifice, a little initiative on my part, but it is well worth it. It is a way I can tell her that I care, that I love her.

Another idea is to send your wife a three-word telegram sometime when you are out of town. Just say, "I LOVE YOU," and leave it unsigned.

When was the last time you brought your wife some flowers? Not for any special occasion, such as a birthday, but just because you love her? Most men have no idea of the meaning of flowers to a woman. We are inclined to think, *Will they last? Will they be useful?* To many women, the very fact that they *aren't* practical and *won't* last give her a special sense of feeling loved just for herself alone.

Sometime when you have to leave early for a breakfast appointment and you are being very quiet so she can sleep in a bit, surprise her with a message on the mirror or tile (written with easily removed soap or eyebrow pencil, please), scrawled in your handwriting, "I love you."

Express your love by doing something nice for her every day. After one marriage seminar Carole and I held, one man's wife was thrilled because he let her out at the church door instead of making her walk from the parking lot. She'd wanted him to do that for her, but for 12 years he stubbornly refused. These are little things, but they speak volumes to a woman's heart.

The third thing I try to do every day is to pay Carole a compliment.

Every day I aim to express some kind of praise—for something she has done which I appreciate, for the way she looks, or, best of all, for who she is.

If your wife has been to the beauty parlor and you don't say anything about how nice her hair looks, you have just passed up a great opportunity to capitalize on your investment. With the cost of hair styling going up all the time, you might as well get the most out of your money.

We often withhold expressions of admiration and thankfulness from those closest to us. The story is told of a taciturn gentleman in Vermont who eventually said to his wife, "When I think of how much you have meant to me all these years, it is almost more than I can do sometimes to keep from telling you so."

The principle here is this: if you like it, say so. Charlie Shedd speaks of the matter of compliments concerning preparing a meal. He says:

> Do you realize, my dear boy, what a tremendous undertaking it is to serve a good meal? Planning, buying, preparing, cooking, setting the table, dishing up, and then the whole messy business in reverse when it's over. In fact, one good meal is such an accomplishment that for you to sit there, devour it, and then hurry on back to your TV game without ever saying a good word must be a mortal sin. Of course I'm not God and I don't know the answer to the old argument about whether there are major and minor evils. But I've had to get up a few meals from beginning to end, and if there is a difference then neglecting to compliment the wife on a good dinner must be a very major error.
>
> There are some instances in which you would be a fool to pass up a 100% return on your investment. This is one of them and just seven words will do: "That was a *great* meal. Thank you!"[1]

When a husband begins to compliment his wife, there is a side benefit other than letting her know you appreciate her. Many wives have told me that, as their husbands compliment them, the children have begun to pick up the habit. They hear Dad compliment Mom, and so little four-year-old Junior begins to do the same thing. So when Mom comes home from the beauty parlor, he says, "Gee, Mom, you look great."

Then after dinner, "Mom, that was a terrific meal." That makes Mom's day. But it is Dad who must set the pace.

So every day . . .

- *speak* your love—tell her that you love her

- *demonstrate* your love by doing something nice for her
- *express* your love by paying her a sincere compliment.

The dividends are outstanding.

NOTES: 1. Charlie Shedd, *Letters to Philip* (Garden City, New York: Doubleday & Company, Inc., 1968), page 24.

19

CHOOSING TO MAKE HER HAPPY
by Jack

I COULDN'T believe what I'd just heard. The group of young adults in our car had been laughing uproariously over some story that had been told when one of the women said wistfully, "I can never remember a time in my growing up years when, as a family, we ever laughed together."

My heart ached for her and for the parents she remembered who were without happiness. In my own life, I have been growing aware of the importance of the habit of happiness for people who are married. We have to cultivate it in ourselves and seek for it in our marriage partner.

I have often asked myself, "Do I have the 'habit of happiness'?" Do I make life exciting around our home? Do my wife and daughter think that it is enjoyable to live in this house with me?

As a husband and leader in our home, it struck me anew that this is *my* responsibility. Now most of us are not comedians. We may not have the capacity to be the life of a continual party in our leisure hours. But there is not one of us who couldn't use his imagination and his creativity to think about things that would produce a "habit of happiness" in his home—something God can and will help us do.

Instead of happiness, many men have honed to a fine point the "habit of gloom." When Dad walks in the door at the end of a tough day, watch out! He is liable to kick the dog first, then verbally kick everyone else in sight after that.

One friend of ours realized that despondency was something that was becoming his lifestyle. He determined to do something about it, and so he mentally started hanging all of his gloom and troubles on a certain telephone pole on his way home from work. The next morning when he went to the office, he'd pull them off the pole and take them to work with him. He told me that it has made a tremendous difference in the evenings around his home.

Christians have something much better to do with burdens than hang them on telephone poles, however. They can give them to Jesus Christ. Peter urged believers to cast "all your anxiety upon Him, because He cares for you" (1 Peter 5:7).

The problem isn't that our wives don't want *to hear* about the burdens with which we wrestle. They are usually quite interested in knowing about them. But it is our *attitude* toward these problems that makes the difference. Do we take out our frustrations on our wives and families, looking defeated and angry, or do we first commit them to the Lord and share with our wives from a vantage point of His peace?

When William Glasser, counselor and author of *Reality Therapy*, was lecturing in Colorado Springs, he stated he would not recommend marrying anyone who had never learned *to laugh*.

We need to develop a sense of humor that will enable

us, at times, to be able to throw back our heads and howl with laughter. Life does have its humorous moments and we must learn to laugh, and to laugh at ourselves also. We all really blunder at times. If we cannot laugh at ourselves, it may indicate that we are taking ourselves too seriously. And taking ourselves too seriously can strain any relationship.

I read an article about resorts in Pennsylvania that cater to honeymooners. Beside the heart-shaped bath-tubs and round beds, most of these resorts have full-time recreational directors. The astounding thing to me was that, according to the story, most of the couples take advantage of a packed schedule that goes on till the wee hours of the morning. The article speculated that the reason for this was that the honeymooners did not know each other well enough yet to know what to say when they were alone, so they kept themselves frantically busy with activity.

It is sad that this could be true with honeymooners. It is tragic that it is true with many couples married several years.

Do you and your mate *enjoy* each other? When you aren't doing anything special? Do you relish your times of just *talking* after the kids have gone to bed? Or is this something you seldom do because you have long since run out of things to say unless it is a sentence during a TV commercial?

When a person is not growing in a relationship with God (see Chapter 13), developing as an individual, stretching to become all that God meant him or her to be, then it isn't the *other* person who is boring. That person is really bored with himself or herself.

Developing an easy, enjoyable, growing relationship takes *work*. It doesn't just happen overnight. Part of that work involves asking God for ideas to develop the habit of happiness. Another is the determination to take time to develop a friendship with each other that is permeated with joy and pleasure in the other's company. This is worth any price it exacts.

Do you know what makes your wife happy? Are you concerned with her happiness? Most of the time it is the little things which count the most. When I asked Carole to name some of the little things she remembered that showed her I really cared, she mentioned that at least once a week when our daughter had colic as a baby, I would sleep on the davenport by her crib to try to help the pain and give Carole a good night's rest. (Wives frequently mention their husband's willingness to babysit so they can go shopping as one of the things they most appreciate about them.)

Carole also mentioned how much she felt loved when, on one birthday when I had to be out of town, she got up to find in a dozen places around the house little "Happy Birthday" messages written with erasable pencil on the TV screen, on the back of the medicine cabinet door, on the mirror in our bathroom, and in many other visible places.

Women have an endless capacity for tenderness, devotion, and love. I have never heard one woman complain about her husband being too considerate. I am wondering if there is any woman anywhere who ever got too much affection.

Most men give a great deal of thought and consideration to details when it comes to their work. If they have a job that is the least bit creative, they are constantly trying to be innovative, to do their jobs better, to come up with new ideas. At work they are creative thinkers. But little of that creativity spills over in improving the love relationship with the person with whom they hope to spend all the years of their lives.

It is vital for a wife to know she is number one in her husband's thinking. We as husbands need to *insure* she knows this to be true. For this we need time and careful thought.

Ask yourself this question: By my actions, how would my wife list these items in order of priority in my life? (Not what I *say*, or how I would list them, but by my *actions* how would my wife see my priorities?) They are scrambled:

1. The ministry in which I am involved
2. My relationship to God
3. My job
4. My wife
5. My children
6. My favorite hobby or sport

After listing these six items in priority order from your vantage point, ask your wife to list these as she sees them prioritized in your life. You may be in for a shock.

A wife needs to be *convinced* that, next to God, she is number one in your thoughts. She can figure out that there is a difference between being number one in *thoughts* and number one in *time.* She obviously cannot be number one in the amount of time you spend with her because you have to spend more hours on your job than you are able to spend with her. In many little ways, however, you communicate to her that she is, or is not, topmost in your thinking.

Carole got a frantic phone call one night at 10 o'clock. It was from a wife who was trying to keep from pushing the panic button. Her husband had not returned home from work yet, and had given her no indication that he was going to be late. She wanted Carole to pray first, then help her decide if she should call the police. Just as her torrent of words poured out, her husband nonchalantly walked in the door. He had effectively communicated to his wife that she was far from being a priority in his thoughts. To her, this incident multiplied many times communicated that her husband simply didn't care.

The neglect of little things, such as letting our wives know when to expect us for dinner, keeping them knowledgeable of our whereabouts, expressing interest in the details of their day, putting their concerns ahead of our own, tell our wives, "You are a low person on my priority list. I don't care about you that much." On the other hand, consistently doing those things which mean so much to her loudly declare, "You are important to me! You are number one! I love you!"

It is essential to demonstrate our love for our wives. To do so is to obey one of God's commandments. May God give us grace to extend our love by words and actions daily, and to prove to our mates that our love has no limits to its expression.

20

CHOOSING TO ACCEPT
by Carole

JACK turned off the light and I lay quietly in the dark, my eyes adjusting to the soft blackness. He was leaving for Colorado the next morning to investigate a change of ministry for us. I knew he was excited, but a bit apprehensive.

I loved our present work in a large city church and had no desire to change. The thought of moving made me tired. Yet a few weeks before, God had nudged me in a very definite way. As I was reading in Deuteronomy (of all places), one verse seemed to glare at me as if lighted in neon. Moses had said, "Behold, the Lord thy God hath set the land before thee; go up and possess it, as the Lord God of thy fathers hath said unto thee, 'Fear not, neither be discouraged' " (1:21).

I said to myself, "Carole, don't take this verse out of context. God said that to the nation Israel."

But the still small Voice refused to be either still or small. My eyes kept being pulled to that one verse as God seemed to say to me, "Carole, take special note of this and be prepared."

I argued back, "I don't want to even *think* You might want us to move, Lord."

138

He responded in my heart, "I said, be ready."

So that evening, several weeks after my talk with the Lord about moving, just as we were about to fall asleep, I quite casually said to Jack, "Honey, if God leads you to take this job, please don't feel you have to wait and ask me about it. I am 100% with you in whatever God leads you to do."

There was a moment of silence. Then Jack gathered me in his arms and with a break in his voice said, "You can't *know* what that means to me!"

From his emotional response, I could tell it meant a great deal. Jack seldom has to choke back tears. And I was reminded for the 101st time how vital it is to a man to *know* his wife is 100% behind him.

As a wife, I have two great fears in my life. One is that I would miss out on some wonderful thing that God has for me because of not being open to it. In the Book of Lamentations God says that His mercies are new every morning and His faithfulness is great (3:23). I surely don't want to miss out on any of the riches that God has for me because I am too lazy or self-centered to search for them.

My second fear is that in some way I might hinder Jack in whatever God has for him to do, defeating him in God's work for his life. While this may be a "healthy fear," it is a scary one. I have watched wives defeat their husbands and in the process destroy them. Solomon said, "An excellent wife is the crown of her husband, but she who shames him is as rottenness in his bones" (Proverbs 12:4). In the Living Bible, that last part reads, "[She] corrodes his strength and tears down everything he does."

Dr. David Hubbard, president of Fuller Theological Seminary, has said, "Marriage does not demand perfection, but it must be given priority. It is an institution for sinners. No one else need apply. But it finds its fullest glory when sinners see it as God's way of leading us to His ultimate curriculum of love and righteousness."[1]

Marriage is "God's way of leading us to His ultimate curriculum." I like that! And there are separate courses for husbands and for wives.

The wife's course is laid out by the Apostle Peter. I like the way the Amplified Bible renders it, for it takes the original Greek word and gives it all of its English meanings. Peter talks about wives having reverent and chaste behaviour, and the word *reverent* in its fuller meaning is described this way: ". . . reverence includes—to respect, defer to, revere him; [revere means] to honor, esteem (appreciate, prize), and [in the human sense] adore him; [and adore means] to admire, praise, be devoted to, deeply love and enjoy [your husband]" (1 Peter 3:2, AMP).

That's all we need to do!

When I first read this list, I threw up my hands in frustration and thought, *No way!* And it is an impossible task . . . except for God. His grace, His power, His enabling is the only way we can ever come close to loving our husbands this way. I am excited about the fact that God never gives us a command that He won't enable us to carry out if we really turn it over to Him. He has commanded that we love our husbands—revere, honor, adore—and He will give us the grace to do it. Some may be thinking, *You don't know my husband!* And that's right, I don't. But God knows him and that promise is not limited by any husband's character.

Love is an expression of our *wills,* not just our feelings. Sometimes only our wills are involved. Many times the feelings will follow an act of our wills to love. A wife may ask, "But isn't it being a hypocrite to tell him I love him when I don't feel any love for him?"

The answer is no. We may need to *will* to love first—to act and talk in a loving way—to *demonstrate* love because we want to obey God.

A woman wrote the following letter to Dr. Clyde Narramore, well-known Christian counselor:

> One day I was saved and I began to know what God could do for me. Was love something that you felt, something that happened to you, or an act of the will? I finally faced the fact that I might not be able to *feel* love, but why could I not *show forth* love? From that moment on I began to behave as if *I did feel love!* What would I do for my husband today, I asked myself, if I really *were* in love with him? Then I proceeded to do these little kindnesses. I studied his likes and dislikes, and bought little treats for his lunchbox. I tried to comfort him when he came home from work tired or harassed by a heavy schedule. I met him at the door with a smile. I respected his discipline of the children and worked with him. I tried to speak softly and diplomatically when we had differences. I listened to him.
>
> Soon, I noticed a marked change in him. He was behaving as though he were living with someone who loved him! And I began to notice a change in my own feelings. He was not at all like I had concluded. He had real depth. And I was beginning to fall in love with him!
>
> Is this why God admonishes us all to show forth love? He has not said to show forth love if you *feel* love, has He? At the time, it seemed to me that Christians did all the giving and none of the getting. But, when God told my heart to show forth love, it was really I who was blessed in the end.[2]

The Holy Spirit will give us a spirit of love flowing

through us. He will give strength to demonstrate love as well as the *feeling* of love. I won't minimize the need for the feeling; it is tremendously important to me. But some wives may need to will to love first and let the feelings come in God's time.

True *acceptance* is perhaps one of the most difficult ways of expressing our love. And one of the most vital.

The first time I heard Jack say that he was the president of the Carole Mayhall Fan Club was at a conference in Colorado where he spoke to the husbands with the wives present. He went on and on about my being a good cook (he thinks I am, but his favorite meal is a pot roast, put in the oven with a can of mushroom soup on it, and cooked to death), a good mother, a good-just-about-everything, which isn't even fractionally true.

As he was saying all those lovely things, you can imagine how it affected me. I was deeply touched. In our room after the meeting, I went to him, put my arms around him, and said, "Thank you for saying such wonderful things about me tonight. But how come you didn't tell them some of the bad things as well?"

He responded, "Because I don't remember any!"

That is acceptance!

Literally speaking, his statements were not true. Jack knows me well. He knows my faults and is aware of some ugly things in my life.

But he accepts me. And I want to accept him in that complete kind of way. It is God's job to make our husbands good. It is our job to make them happy. And one of the ways we can make them most happy is by accepting them.

John Powell tells of talking to a friend while he was writing his book *why am i afraid to tell you who i am?* The friend said, "Do you want an answer to your question?"

The author replied, "Well, that's the purpose of the book, to answer the question."

So his friend said, "But do you want *my* answer?"

John Powell said he did.

So his friend said, "I am afraid to tell you who I am, because, if I tell you who I am, you may not like who I am, and it's all that I have."[3]

Most people will not be open with us unless they feel accepted. They can risk vulnerability only if they know they are accepted with all their faults, hangups, and idiosyncrasies. Acceptance is *felt*.

We might ask, How many "why" questions do you use each day with the person to whom you are married? Have you ever considered that a "why" question is threatening and that it may be an indication of how much or how little you are truly accepting? I am not talking about information type "why" questions, but questions such as, Why did you turn there? Why are you late? Why did you forget your raincoat? Why wouldn't you let me go? Why did you do it that way? These are all the type of questions which shouts, "I wouldn't have turned there, been late, forgotten my raincoat, done it that way." You may not *mean* the question to suggest that (though it just could be that you did), but that is the way such questions often come across.

One winter our cable TV went out on the set in our bedroom. After calling the repairman for two weeks with no results, Jack ingeniously ran a long wire down the hall and hooked up another cable so we could have a picture on our bedroom set.

One Saturday afternoon the repairman showed up, and as I answered his ring, he abruptly asked, "Do you have a picture?"

Well, we *did* have a picture, but only thanks to my

husband's genius and an ugly wire running the entire length of the hallway. I answered the repairman's question before I explained the whole situation by saying, "Yes . . . "

Jack heard this from the upstairs hallway and, realizing what the repairman *meant*, interrupted our conversation. "No," he said, "we don't have a picture." He then proceeded to show the man what had happened.

As he was following the man outside, going back and forth, Jack walked through the kitchen and said, "Why did you tell him we had a picture?" Without pausing long enough for me to say *anything*, he went outside.

As the saying goes, I stood there with egg on my face! I felt immediately and giantly . . . stupid. And hurt.

My head was saying logically, "Carole, Jack did not mean to hurt you," but my heart was saying, "Ouch." A great, big chunk of ice lay between what my head was saying and what my heart was feeling.

His "why" question had done it.

Now (just so you'll have the ending to this incident), I am learning not to harbor hurt feelings. So as Jack was rushing through again, I stopped him. "I am feeling very stupid as a result of what you said," I managed to get out.

"What did I say?" he inquired with great concern. (I *knew* he hadn't meant it deliberately.)

When I told him, he quickly apologized. "Honey, I didn't mean to hurt you. I'm sorry. Will you forgive me?"

That big block of ice melted—there wasn't even a puddle left.

A good checkup on your AQ (Acceptance Quotient) is to see if you can go a whole week without asking an intimidating "why" question . . . then a whole month . . . and then strike it from your vocabulary altogether. The elimination of threatening questions can be a practical means of helping your loved ones feel your acceptance. And in acceptance, freedom. And in freedom, love.

NOTES: 1. Dr. David Hubbard, used by permission.
2. From *A Woman's World* by Dr. Clyde M. Narramore, page 148. Copyright © 1963 by Zondervan Publishing House. Used by permission.
3. John Powell, *why am i afraid to tell you who i am?* (Niles, Illinois: Argus Communications, 1969), page 12.

21

CHOOSING TO APPRECIATE
by Carole

CISCO, Utah. Mentally my mind said it, *Ceēzco*, the way the Cisco Kid's sidekick used to pronounce it in the western movies many long years ago.

And "Ceēzco" looked just like it sounded. Bypassed by the Interstate many years before, all that remained of the town were four weatherbeaten shells of former motels, the skeletons of two filling stations, hulks of old houses, and Ethel's Cafe.

We pulled up in front of Ethel's to meet our fellow rafters to begin a two-day white-water trip through the canyons of Utah.

I thought about Cisco and our exciting day as I lay staring into the black sky that night. I pulled my sleeping bag (more appropriately termed my "lying awake" bag) over my side and wiggled to find a more comfortable position on my tiny back-pad.

This was a trip I'd wanted to take for years and God had finally arranged it . . . with our daughter, her husband, and several other special friends. We were on an adventure trip which proved to be, as Lynn later put it, "One which met all our expectations and none of our fears." It was great.

I looked over at Jack, sleeping beside me, and a great wave of feeling engulfed me. I wanted to wake him up, throw my arms around him, and say, "Hey, I *appreciate* you." It had been my enthusiasm which had fanned the trip-flame, but it took Jack's love and consideration to make it possible. I took a few minutes to thank the Lord for a husband who gives of himself.

What exactly is appreciation?

A few years ago we moved to Colorado after being in the Chicago area for 14 years. We had formed some deep friendships in those 14 years, and I found after moving that I was lonely. I went through a period of six months of rather difficult adjustment to our new situation.

This adjustment caused me to realize that my mother had moved about the same time of her life. Shortly after his three children had left home to be married or to go to college, Daddy had changed jobs. Mother went from a town where she was well known in the community, away from a church in which she was active and knew everyone, left a large old rambling home she loved, and moved into a little crackerbox-house in another state where she knew no one. Yet I never heard her complain.

When I went to visit my mother after our move, I asked her about *her* move. I described our similar state of affairs in moving, my loneliness, and then said, "Mom, I never heard one word of complaint or grumbling from you. How come?"

Mother's eyes widened in surprise, and she looked shocked by my question. She said, "Why Carole, I was with your *father!*" *That* is appreciation.

Mrs. Norman Vincent Peale has said:

> Every person needs to feel that he marches at the head of some other person's parade, that his happiness and welfare

come first, ahead of all happiness and welfares. This sense of being able to claim complete priority in another person's affections is the cornerstone of marriage, but the only way a person can be sure he has this priority is when the other person sends clear, frequent, unambiguous signals confirming it. It is not enough to love someone routinely or passively or mutely.[1]

Jack and I were sitting in a coffee shop one afternoon, discussing the question of priorities. He asked me how I knew I was number one after God on his priority list. I recalled several incidents that more than proved to me my status in his life, such as the time he canceled a business trip to take care of me when I had caught the mumps from our daughter Lynn and was very ill. I looked like a horror at the time, but he didn't even comment on my grotesque appearance, which added saintliness to his virtues.

When I asked his question back to him, he said, "I know that I am on the top of your priority list because *you tell me.* I may not be greatly responsive when you compliment me [sometimes he acts embarrassed, or responds in a more subdued way than I would], but I really appreciate all the nice things you say."

Solomon stated that "a man hath joy by the answer of his mouth and a word spoken in due season, how good is it" (Proverbs 15:23, KJV).

Joy comes into our lives and marriages as we learn to speak many "good words" to those we love, but especially to that one God has chosen to be our partner for life.

NOTES: 1. Mrs. Norman Vincent Peale, used by permission.

22

CHOOSING TO ADMIRE
by Carole

"I REALLY don't like this restaurant," my friend murmured under her breath. "But it's one of Bill's favorites." It was quickly obvious that it was not one of hers.

As we dined that evening, I thought the old world atmosphere delightful, the food good, and the service excellent. But from the barrage of disparaging comments, it became blatantly apparent that we were here only because Bill had chosen it over his wife's disapproval. She had made up her mind not to like that restaurant, and not even Maxim's of Paris would have pleased her that summer evening.

The signals she telegraphed were clearly sent and pointedly received. She did not approve of her husband. Yes, I said, of her *husband*. She may have thought she was criticizing a restaurant, but her verbal stabs at the food, the noise, and the service were aimed with accuracy at his taste, his choice, his manners. And she was drawing blood.

Inwardly I thought, *Oh, please, don't.* In our women's group, we had been studying ways to encourage our husbands, and one of the most effective ways to encourage is by expressing admiration . . . to encourage and build instead of "corroding his strength and tearing down everything he does" (Proverbs 12:4, LB). One of the greatest ministries a wife can have in her husband's life is the ministry of encouragement through admiration. Not flattery, but sincere praise. My friend was striving to build—but she had just torn away several months of effort . . . and probably wasn't even aware of what she had done.

The most objective man I know becomes totally subjective when his wife belittles him or expresses disapproval of something he has chosen, be it a restaurant or a gift.

I can almost hear someone saying, "But what if I don't *like* what he has given me or the restaurant he has chosen? Isn't it *wrong* to be dishonest and say that I like it when I don't?"

Another friend of mine learned a valuable lesson in this area. Her husband was not yet a Christian, and she had been trying to show Christ's love to him. They had had some major problems in the years before she invited Christ to take over her life. Then, for her birthday, he had given her some bathroom towels. She didn't think that was a very personal gift and was disappointed; she hated the color of the towels (she is a warm orange-yellow-red person, and the color he chose was beige), and when she asked him if he minded if she exchanged them for another color, he had said, "Yes, I do mind." Period.

Now how was she in all honesty supposed to be grateful for those towels?

God taught her something through that incident. As she prayed about it, God reminded her of the years her husband hadn't given her *any* remembrance on her birthday. This year, he had made the effort to shop, buy, and wrap a present for her. She *was* appreciative of that. So while she couldn't honestly rave over beige towels, she could and did express warm gratitude for the love and time of her husband (and she bought bright colored washcloths to go with the towels).

That is one wise woman.

Perhaps the old saying "If you can't think of something nice to say, don't say anything" is a good one to follow in situations like this. If you have gone out to eat at a real "bummer," and nothing is right except the water and even that is served in a dirty glass, the important thing is for the other person to know that you are glad to be *with him.* All else can be ignored. Your husband is not dumb enough to take you there again, anyhow.

Many questions puzzle our minds when it comes to expressing admiration to our husbands. Here are some of the most common.

One question that is asked often is: Won't it make my husband proud if I keep complimenting and admiring him?

The answer is no. The Bible says, "Do not withhold good from those to whom it is due, when it is in your power to do it" (Proverbs 3:27). Sincere praise costs little. If it is "in the power of your hand to do it" (AMP), then God says not to withhold it. So you are disobeying God when you fail to compliment and encourage your husband (and others as well). I can never thank the Lord enough for a mother and father who constantly affirmed me. I didn't believe them when they told this gangling girl with braces on her teeth that she was beautiful, but it certainly built security and a feeling of being loved into my life. And I guess to them, I *was* beautiful. Their esteem didn't make me proud—except of my great parents.

We all long for admiration. Women tend to compliment other women and receive admiration from their small children. But men seldom praise each other. Perhaps this is why they have a greater need along this line. But a man hungers for admiration, and it is vital to him. And if *you* are not the source of the encouragement he needs, someone else may be.

Another frequent and searching question is: I'm always complimenting my husband, but he continues to cut me down. I don't have any resources left—I can't go on. What do I do?

No easy answer exists for this one.

A wife once asked me, "What do you do when you have knocked yourself out preparing a good meal for your husband and he says, 'That was the lousiest meal I've ever eaten'?"

I almost responded with, "Cry a lot," but that wouldn't have helped her.

She went on to explain that she really tried to show her husband how much she loved him and tried to compliment him, but he kept cutting her down. She was just too tired to keep on trying.

As we talked, she admitted that her husband had a low self image and didn't like himself or think he was any good. So I asked her if, when she complimented him, she thought he really *heard* her. After considering this question, she answered, "No, he probably doesn't hear me."

Many people have such a low estimation of themselves that they simply sluff off any compliment given them. But they pick up in flashing neon lights any slight, slur, complaint, or negative tone of voice. Then, in order to try to build themselves up, they put others down, especially their wives. The cycle spirals ever downward.

Someone has to break into that vicious cycle, and it can be the Christian wife. The first thing she may have to do is to ask a creative God for ideas on how to express admiration for her husband in a way that he will hear. To pray that God will open inroads to his heart and give him a God-confidence, so that he will have a greater self-confidence. It will take time and patience. But our God is a miracle-working God.

As we continued talking, I suggested to this wife that she pray for ideas on how to get through to her husband, whom she sincerely loved and admired . . . new ways that she hadn't tried before. Ways such as never failing to tell him a "third person compliment." Wives should never miss the opportunity of telling their husbands nice things someone else has said about them.

Another way is to start with compliments he might really believe. If a wife told her overweight husband that she admired his physique, he may think she was putting him on even if she were sincere; but if she told him how much she appreciated the way he worked so hard to provide for her and the children, he might believe her. She could also express admiration in non-verbal ways. At the heart and core of this is the physical expression of love. A wife can defeat every nice remark she has made all day if she is not wholehearted in making her husband feel like a man in bed at night. (More on this in a later chapter.) But many wives have given up on even the little expressions of love such as greeting him at the door with a kiss and a smile, being dressed up just for him, planning special dinners—things you have heard about all your life but are inclined to let slide after several years of marriage.

Have you convinced your husband that his coming
home is the high point of your day?

In her book *One Plus One Equals One*, Kay Arvin
describes the negative of that situation:

> Charles said it well, simply and clearly. "You know,
> when I get home after work, the only one who acts as if she
> cares at all is my little dog. She really is glad to see me and
> lets me know it. Maybe everybody is, I don't know. But you
> can't tell it. I always come in the back door because Doris is
> in the kitchen about then, usually. But she always looks up
> from whatever she is doing with the most startled look, and
> says, 'Oh, are you home already?' She says it like she really
> means, 'Surely you're not home already!' Somehow she
> makes me feel like I've done the wrong thing, just by get-
> ting home. I used to try and say hello to the kids, but I don't
> do that anymore. Seems I would get in between them and
> the TV set at just the wrong minute, and the darn thing was
> so loud they couldn't hear what I said anyway—when
> they were home, that is, which they usually weren't. So
> now, I just pick up little Suzy, my dog, stick her under my
> arm and go out in the yard. I act like I don't care, and maybe
> I shouldn't really—but I do. It gives me the feeling that all I
> am hanging around there for is just to pay the bills and keep
> the place up. You know, I believe that if the bills were taken
> care of and nothing broke, I bet I could be gone a whole
> week and nobody would even notice it."
>
> Charles felt like stomping his feet and yelling, "Hey,
> please somebody, look happy just a little that I've come
> home again. Don't shut me out. Doggone it, I'm glad to be
> here; somebody be glad with me." But he was an uncompli-
> cated, well-mannered man, and instead of stomping and
> yelling, he quietly swallowed his hurt, took the little dog
> under his arm, and went out into the backyard to play with

her. The hurt pride didn't disappear though but followed the course of many small hurts which, through repetition, grew into resentment.[1]

Our marriages rest on such things!

It became apparent as I talked to the wife whose husband had criticized her meal so cruelly that her idea of being a godly wife was never to express a negative feeling. It was no wonder she was coming apart at the seams. Her anger had as many quills as a porcupine and she was unconsciously sending them to stick in her husband's flesh. No, she hadn't *told* him how his cutting remarks were hurting her. She wasn't even letting her husband *know* her—not the real inside vulnerable part of her, anyway.

In *love*, she needed to tell her husband how she felt when he made a remark like, "That was the lousiest meal I ever ate." It hurt her. It made her feel like giving up and never cooking meals again. It tore her apart and made her want to chew nails. So she should tell him . . . but in love.

Now God *is* concerned with *how* we express ourselves. He says, "It is better to dwell in a corner of the housetop [on the flat oriental roof, exposed to all kinds of weather] than in a house shared with a nagging, quarrelsome *and* faultfinding woman" (Proverbs 21:9, AMP). And very descriptively Solomon said, "As a ring of gold in a swine's snout, so is a beautiful woman who lacks discretion" (Proverbs 11:22). Discretion to me means knowing when to speak and when to keep quiet. I wish I had more discretion!

How can we express a negative in a positive way? Many books have been written about how to do it, but one of the most helpful truths that I have picked up from them is expressing our feelings in "I" statements, "I am feeling hurt and angry," rather than the accusatory "you" statements, "You make me mad when you do that." In order to be faithful to our husbands and to ourselves, we must be honest, but we need love and wisdom to be honest in the right way. "Never forget to be truthful and kind. Hold these virtues tightly. Write them deep within your heart" (Proverbs 3:3, LB). And always there should be the positive, "Anxiety in the heart of a man weights it down, but a good word makes it glad" (Proverbs 12:25). If we surround our husbands with praise and admiration, and if we build up an atmosphere and climate of love and appreciation, a small squall on the horizon isn't going to do anything but clear the air. But if the weather isn't usually sunny, then a cloudburst can wash away many good words.

So, if your husband has a habit of cutting you down continually, remember these four things:

1. Ask God for ideas to get through to him that you sincerely love and admire him.

2. Pray that God would change his heart and give him a more positive self-image so that he can respond lovingly to you.

3. Be honest in your feelings and "speak the truth in love."

4. Ask God for the strength to keep on loving and admiring him till you break into and reverse that downward cycle of ego-destruction.

Another question frequently heard is: How do I admire and encourage my husband in practical ways?

Some suggested answers are:

1. Pray every day for the ability to be an encourager. Ask God for opportunities to say that "good word"—not just to your husband, but to everyone you meet. God can

use this ability to make you a complete breath of blessing to those around you and the dividends are way out of proportion to the time invested.

2. Keep a list of how other women show admiration for their husbands. Paul said that the older women are to teach the younger women to "love their husbands" (Titus 2:4). Now I don't know how anyone can teach another to *feel* love, so I take this to mean that the older women (both spiritually and in age) should teach the younger women to *demonstrate* love for their husbands. Make a point to ask older women how they express love. Ask your husband in what ways you are an encouragement to him, and then ask him for his suggestions as to how you might be more of an encouragement to him.

3. Compliment him every day. Some books will tell you that a man prefers to be complimented for his "manly" characteristics, such as his physical strength and ability to lead. But I really doubt that there is anything that a man would *resent* in the way of a sincere compliment. Remember, too, to repeat compliments from others.

4. Be a grateful wife—accept his gifts with love and pleasure.

5. And remember, if you *don't* admire your husband, then ask God for a truly loving, admiring heart and start *acting* like you thought he was wonderful. Feelings often follow actions. If we waited for the feelings, many of us would never act.

Our husbands need to know, feel, and *be* the number one person in our lives. God grant that it be so.

NOTES: 1. Kay K. Arvin, *One Plus One Equals One*, pages 37-38. © Copyright 1969 Broadman Press, Nashville, Tennessee. All rights reserved. Used by permission.

23

CHOOSING TO GROW
by Jack

I CAME in the front door whistling, pausing to hang my jacket in the hall closet. Usually, Carole would come from some part of the house to greet me when I arrived home from work, but this night all I heard were small sounds coming from the kitchen. The year was 1956.

"Hi, honey," I called through the length of the house.

"Hello," came the response from the recesses of the kitchen.

The chill in her tone signaled that something was wrong. *What have I done now?* I wondered.

Optimistically, I thought I might be able to avoid a quarrel, so I walked into the kitchen, gave Carole a quick hug, and forcing cheerfulness, asked, "Have a good day?"

"Yes," came her monotoned response. (Translation: "I haven't, and it's all your fault!")

"Anything wrong?" I queried.

"No," she answered. (Translation: "You have to ask me some more before I'll tell you.")

We had been married a few years and these clashes had formed a pattern. I would do something that Carole didn't like, and she would withdraw in cold silence till I finally asked enough times to find out what the problem was. Then, none too gently, she would tell me.

Since I had a temper also, I would snap back and defend myself, or be silently hostile. Fortunately, Carole gets over her anger quickly once she has told me her feelings, and she would apologize, or I would, and things would be peaceful again.

Our problem was that the conflicts were becoming more frequent and violent and we could not fathom either the cause or find the solution. The result was a great deal of frustration in both of us.

But that evening, though neither of us can remember what the initial dispute was about, we remember that God took charge in a way we hadn't anticipated.

"I know there is something bothering you. Tell me what it is," I persisted.

She told me then, in detail, and in anger.

I was ready to lash back. But instead, God spoke through a verse which I had learned that week. "Jack, *you* have need of patience, that, after you have done the will of God, you might receive the promise" (Hebrews 10:36, KJV).

At once, I felt a love and tenderness toward Carole that was not at all like me in these kinds of heated situations, and I heard myself saying, "Well, you are right. I'm sorry. Why don't we pray about it together?"

Carole, shocked, was silent. And I *did* pray. The next moment her arms were around me and she was saying, "I'm sorry too, honey. Please forgive me."

In a graphic way that evening, both of us saw how learning Scripture is *life* changing and *habit* changing.

I hadn't been memorizing Scripture for long. A few weeks prior to this incident, I'd had lunch with Skip

Gray, Navigator representative in the area, and in the course of talking about some things I'd heard at a conference, he pulled out a little packet of cards which had Bible verses printed on them. Over the lunch hour, he offered to give me the packet *if* I would memorize the four verses it contained. So I rose to the challenge, took the packet, and memorized the four verses. When I knew the four verses word-perfect, I met Skip again the following week, and he checked me out on them.

Then he said, "Why don't you enroll in the Topical Memory System of The Navigators?[1] It will help you learn how to memorize Scripture."

I did enroll and at the time of our quarrel had memorized a number of verses which were planted firmly in my heart. When Carole told me what I had done that morning to hurt her, the Spirit of God took one of those verses and applied it to my life. How grateful I am that He did.

This was our first real encounter with what God's Word could do in a real, live situation on a moment's notice. And it was the beginning of a brand new dimension in our marriage relationship. Carole realized the difference God's Word was beginning to make in my life and it wasn't long before she began to memorize some verses also. As both of us applied these Scriptures to our lives, God began to change us in practical, shoe-leather ways.

For the time invested, there is *no other way* of getting the Word of God into our lives that has more meaning, is more life changing, and has more significance than memorizing verses and passages from the Bible—putting them in our hearts for the Spirit of God to use. This is still a continual source of help to me as I have made it a habit of life.

Polls have shown that the average Christian, regardless of how long he or she has been a Christian, has memorized, with references, 12 verses of Scripture. How tragic that is. The resources of God can be just a thought away, but instead lie buried in His Book. If you were to memorize only one verse a week and review these verses regularly, in one year your life would be enriched by 52 verses which God could use anywhere, anytime. That is over four times what most Christians know. And there is not one of you who couldn't do it.

Scripture verses do have to be reviewed once we have learned them. Our minds are similar to a grassy yard in a corner lot. If the lot is on the way to the local school and the kids start taking a shortcut across it in order to get to school three seconds sooner, the first few days their steps will not be noticed. But in a couple of weeks, a path will become visible and in a month only bare dirt will remain.

When we put something through our minds enough times, it is going to wear a pathway in our brain that will remain. We remember our phone numbers and our addresses because of constant repetition. So it is with memorizing Scripture.

God has said through the Apostle Paul:

> I urge you therefore, brethren, by the mercies of God, to present your bodies a living and holy sacrifice, acceptable to God, which is your spiritual service of worship. And do not be conformed to this world, but be transformed by the renewing of your mind, that you may prove what the will of God is, that which is good and acceptable and perfect (Romans 12:1-2).

Being conformed to this world is a *process* which takes

place over a long period of time. Having our minds "renewed by God" is also a process which takes place by us allowing our minds to be influenced by the way God thinks—which is written down in the pages of His Word. The more we expose our thinking to His Word, the more our minds are remade from within and we begin to think on parallel lines with God. If we want God to change us "from one degree of glory to another" (2 Corinthians 3:18, AMP), if we want to be conformed to the image of His Son, if we want to become the kinds of husbands and wives who will grow in love and godliness, an excellent way to progress is by allowing God to invade our lives through His Word as *we learn it by heart*.

NOTES: 1. *The Topical Memory System* and other Navigator memory materials are available from your local Christian bookstore.

SECTION V

Responsibilities

24

CHOOSING TO LEAD
by Jack

Con·fu·sion /kən-ˈfyü-zhən/ *n* **1:** an act or instance of confusing **2:** the quality or state of being confused.[1]

GENERALLY speaking, the husband's responsibility in the home today is in a state of confusion.

Colonel Baron George Von Trapp whistles a series of signals and his children tumble down the stairs, line up in descending order by age, and stand at attention while an astonished Maria looks on. Some men seem to look on this scene from "Sound of Music" as the way to be the biblical heads of their homes. They are confused about what constitutes biblical leadership.

Contractual marriage is being touted among certain groups in our society today. The adherents claim that to sign a marriage contract which spells out all responsibilities and decisions, splitting them equally between the man and the woman will lead to freedom and harmony. They are confused about what constitutes a biblical marriage.

Distorted views are making the rounds these days on the subject of leadership within Christian marriage. Many are arguing with God's plan; some do not really understand it; others don't want to believe it. They are confused.

What is God's plan for leadership in a marriage? What does the term *headship* mean?

I remember as a boy being fascinated by our county fair. I loved it all—the crowds, the grandstand show, the exhibits—but most of all I enjoyed the midway with its rides and sideshows. At one fair, the big attraction at one of the sideshows was a two-headed monster. Paying my dime (that's how long ago it was!), I went in and was at the same time horrified and fascinated to see a cow with a second head growing out of its neck at an angle. It was grotesque.

A two-headed *anything* is a mistake of nature and is considered a freak. And two heads in a marriage relationship is no different. God is not in the business of making monsters. He created the marriage union with one head only.

In my work, I've had the opportunity to make several detailed studies on leadership, and the information I obtained has helped me understand both the responsibilities of leadership and the principles involved in being a leader. The responsibilities are awesome and the principles are difficult. I'd just as soon abdicate at times, but to do so would be to disobey God. For His Word has clearly stated, "The husband is the head of the wife, as Christ also is the head of the church, He Himself being the Saviour of the body. But the church is subject to Christ, so also the wives ought to be to their husbands in everything" (Ephesians 5:23-24). Some people try desperately to run around this passage of Scripture. However, it must be faced head on and reckoned with as part of God's overall plan for marriage.

The husband is to be the head, the leader of his wife.

The Bible states that this is to be a leadership of love, and love and authority are intertwined in this passage. Leadership without love usually results in tyranny; but in marriage, love without leadership leads to unstable, fanciful romanticism. A right balance of responsible authority and unselfish love must be maintained. Difficult? Yes. Impossible really without the wisdom and strength of the Holy Spirit.

BASIC RESPONSIBILITIES

In my study of leadership, I discovered that the two basic responsibilities of any leader are to watch out for the welfare of his people and to accomplish the mission or goals on which the people have decided. God has given us a beautiful example of leadership in the life of David. "He also chose David His servant, and took him from the sheepfolds; from the care of the ewes with suckling lambs He brought him, to shepherd Jacob His people, and Israel His inheritance. So he [David] shepherded them according to the integrity of his heart, and guided them with his skillful hands" (Psalm 78:70-72). David cared for his people—he watched out for their welfare—and he guided them to accomplish the goals that God had given.

For a husband to be a godly leader of his home, both of these responsibilities need to be kept in mind. It is his job to watch out for his wife and children and to guide his family with skill in those goals which they have purposed together to achieve.

What *are* your goals as a husband and wife? Have you ever talked about them or written them down—both short range and long range? What is it that you want to accomplish in the next year, five years, ten years as the result of your lives and marriage?

If you have never done so, take a weekend alone with your wife away from everyone and spend some time praying and talking over goals and objectives for your lives together. Plan ahead what you will talk about so that you don't drift. God will give you direction as you talk with Him and with one another.

One long-range goal worth considering is to exemplify Christ in your home, to create such an environment and atmosphere in your relationship together that your love will be a picture of Christ's love for His church, to manifest in your home the fruits of the Holy Spirit, which are love, joy, peace, longsuffering, gentleness, goodness, meekness, faith (Galatians 5:22-23). This is a lifetime goal worth working for. This goal will then need to be broken up into bite-sized portions by shorter range goals, perhaps doing some topical Bible studies on each of these characteristics with your family, discussing with them ways of demonstrating love in everyday life.

The Prophet Malachi suggests another goal to consider (see Malachi 2:13-16). He talks about what is on the Lord's heart for us and sums it up in two words—*godly offspring*. I believe this means both physical children and spiritual children—those we have led to Christ or "adopted" as God has directed us. To produce godly offspring takes sacrifice, determination, and prayer. But is there a more worthy goal?

It has been said that there are two things from our present world that are going to last forever. These are the Word of God and people. "Heaven and earth will pass away, but My words shall not pass away," Jesus told us (Matthew 24:35). The Word of God will endure forever.

And people will last for eternity. "For God so loved the world, that He gave His only begotten Son, that whoever believes in Him should not perish, but have eternal life" (John 3:16). We should invest our lives in that which is eternal . . . which will bring eternal rewards. Paul exemplified the joy of doing this when he said to the Thessalonians: "For who is our hope or joy or crown of exultation? Is it not even you, in the presence of our Lord Jesus at His coming? For you are our glory and joy" (1 Thessalonians 2:19-20).

It is the responsibility of the husband to watch out for the welfare of his wife and children, and to insure that he and his wife are accomplishing, as a couple, those goals for which God has put them together.

PRINCIPLES OF GOOD LEADERSHIP

In the vast amount of research done on the subject of leadership, it has been discovered that leaders who practiced certain principles were successful no matter what their fields might have been. But leaders who were not successful constantly violated these same principles.

That research says quite a bit to me. While these are not hard and fast rules, leadership principles are good guidelines and are certainly applicable to a husband who wants to be a loving leader of his family. We want to explore a few of these principles in this and the next chapters. I am trying with the help of God to practice them.

PRINCIPLE NUMBER ONE—*Know your wife in order to look out for her welfare.* Most men simply do not *know* their wives. Take the following brief quiz by mentally answering these five questions:
- What is your wife's greatest concern right now?
- What is her greatest need?
- What is her wildest dream?

- What is her smallest pain?
- What new vista would she like to explore?

Can you answer these questions with certainty? If not, you don't, at the moment, *know* your wife. And if you don't know her, it will be very difficult for you to look out for her welfare. Perhaps she needs physical rest or time away from the children. Or she has a spiritual need and needs to pray with you. She may need encouragement; she may need to be *noticed* because she has been feeling like a part of your landscape you are not seeing. She may need an understanding heart, a listening ear, a word of appreciation, a new dress, a diverting interest, to share in a recreational hobby or sport with you, or a vacation. You may be saying, "Whatever it is, I can't afford it." But if you want to be God's kind of husband, you can't afford *not* to know and try to meet that need that she may have in her life.

PRINCIPLE NUMBER TWO—*Keep the channels of communication open and clear*. The lack of a deep level of communication is the recognized number one problem in most marriages. And clear communication is vital to the success and growth of a marriage. It is not only important in knowing one another, it is essential for the high morale of your entire family. If you want a happy wife, take the responsibility for communicating on a depth level with her, to let her know what is going on in your *innermost* person.

Paul tells us that husbands are to love their wives in the same way as Christ loved the church (Ephesians 5:25), and to lead their wives in that way too. Now who took the initiative in communicating—Christ or the church? Christ took the initiative to open doors of communication with His people. If husbands are to exemplify Christ, then it is their responsibility to take the initiative in communicating clearly.

Carole and I have the opportunity to present some of these principles in marriage seminars in many parts of the country from time to time. We hear a common complaint from wives as we talk about the matter of communication. They say that their husbands not only fail to initiate communication, but they are reluctant to cooperate even when their wives suggest it. Many of these husbands would be aghast if they were told that they were disobeying *God* in this lack of initiative and cooperation. We then suggest some practical assignments and questions[2] to these couples to stimulate their exploring each other's hearts.

So know your wife and communicate clearly with her. It is your responsibility. You can't know her unless you *do* communicate, so these two principles go hand in hand. Through God's help, you can grow and mature together.

NOTES: 1. By permission. From *Webster's New Collegiate Dictionary.* © 1977 by G. & C. Merriam Co., Publishers of the Merriam-Webster Dictionaries, page 238.

2. The assignments we give are selected questions from the *Discussion Questions for Better Communication,* found at the end of this book, beginning with page 231.

25

CHOOSING TO SOLVE PROBLEMS
by Jack

SEVERAL years ago, The Navigators asked me to move into a job which meant traveling much of the time. This travel caused a problem which I did not recognize immediately, but soon caused major irritations which became apparent to both Carole and me.

I would be on a trip for a couple of weeks. All the time I was away, I was with people. People, people, people, people, till I was up to my frustration level with talking, interacting, helping with problems, and dealing in ministry situations. When I got home, I was weary of talking.

On the other hand, Carole had been home, conversing mostly with our 10-year-old daughter. The moment I walked in the front door, after greeting me enthusiastically, Carole wanted to *hear all* about the trip. Often she would want to go out to dinner in order to get out of the house and spend the entire evening talking.

The first two or three times this happened it ended up with us spending the whole evening trying to resolve the problem. I would become angry because she didn't understand how I felt, and she was irritated at my not understanding her needs. The third time I got back from a trip, she had invited some friends over for dinner on the night of my return. That popped the cork off the bottle as far as I was concerned.

After several go-rounds, we began to realize we had a "generic problem." In this sense *generic* means "long-range, repetitive, happening again and again." Webster defines it, "Relating to or characteristic of a whole group or class."[1] It was going to keep on happening because I was going to keep on traveling and, hopefully, I was going to keep on coming home and Carole would be there waiting. So unless something was done about our generic problem, it was going to continue to create greater and greater tensions.

Recognizing the problem is only half the battle. So, when we saw what was happening time after time, we sat down to talk about it, in between two trips when we were both more objective. I expressed to Carole how I felt after being away two weeks, that I was exhausted mentally and physically, and all I wanted to do was sit and stare at the ceiling, have a good home-cooked meal, and get a good night's sleep in my own bed. She explained how she felt, feeling left out of two weeks of my life, not too much adult companionship while I was gone, and interested and anxious to hear what I had been doing.

In this discussion, we *heard* each other and endeavored to find a solution which turned out to be quite simple. As we prayed about it together, a compromise came to us that met both of our needs. The first night I was home, our guideline stated, we would never have company for dinner, and unless I felt like talking about the trip or part of it, Carole wouldn't ask about it. This enabled me to come home, flop and unwind, watch a little TV, read, or just go to bed. But within 24 hours, I accepted the responsibility to sit down with Carole, tell her *all* about the trip, answer *any* of the questions she might have, and many times take her out for dinner. We haven't had a problem with this type of thing since working out those guidelines.

Generic problems need generic solutions. And the husband is obligated to see that the difficulties are thought through *together*.

Some common generic problems arise from the distribution of work around the house when a wife works outside the home. These may be problems concerning money management, especially if the couple's spending style is 180° opposite from one another, priorities in time (if one is a workaholic and the other a sports nut, for instance), and even how to spend holidays and vacations.

Every couple will find themselves faced with generic problems frequently—the same thing is going to come up next month that you faced today. The couple must discuss the problems *together*, come up with creative solutions *together*, and work on those solutions *together*. But the responsibility lies with the *husband*, the leader in the home, to be alert to these problems and insure that there is discussion concerning them. It does not matter who initiates this discussion, but the accountability before God rests on the husband to make sure a solution is talked about and worked out.

Didn't I say that leadership isn't easy?

NOTES: 1. By permission, From *Webster's New Collegiate Dictionary*. © 1977 by G. & C. Merriam Co., Publishers of the Merriam-Webster Dictionaries, page 478.

26

CHOOSING HEADSHIP
by Jack

"YOU WON'T believe this, folks," Lynn, our daughter, wrote from college, "but my room is the neatest on the whole floor."

She was right on two counts—it *was* the neatest room on the floor and we had an extremely difficult time believing it.

In Lynn's growing years, Carole and I had tried every means we could think of to get Lynn to keep her room orderly. But somehow *her* idea of a clean room and *our* idea of it weren't even on speaking terms.

She confided to us later in her first year of college, "I guess I was just so used to seeing things picked up that I couldn't stand a mess." And now she wins the blue ribbon for order in her own home.

The best method of teaching and of leading is *to set an example*, which brings us to:

PRINCIPLE NUMBER THREE—*Set an example*. It is impossible for a husband to ask or expect his wife and family to do something that he doesn't consider important enough to do himself.

Are you an example to your family in having a consistent time with God each day? Do you memorize God's Word? Do you study it? Are you hospitable, courteous, and honest? Whatever virtue you may want to see in your children has got to begin with you.

The phone rings late on Friday evening. Junior answers it, and it's for Dad. Now Dad has had one of the worst weeks in years. He's absolutely exhausted and mad at the whole world. Without thinking, he says, "Tell him I'm not here." Honesty will never be established as a value in that home if Dad has no integrity. The responsibility and privilege of husbands is to set an example.

PRINCIPLE NUMBER FOUR—*Make sound and timely decisions.* Make them; don't abdicate them. To make good decisions takes much thought and work, but they are absolutely vital. A businessman told me that he can hire people to do everything but two things—think and do things in the order of their importance.

But God will help us think. One of the tremendous assets of being in touch with God through Jesus Christ is that He will help us in making our decisions. The Lord has promised us in His Word that He will instruct us and guide us in the way that we should go. He will guide us with His eye being on us (Psalm 32:8). Many times a decision boils down to determining together what the will of God *is.* What does He want us to do in this situation? The road may have only one fork in it, or there may be a dozen things involved in the decision. But God has a way for us to go.

Scripture contains many concrete instructions—the "thou shalts" and the "thou shalt nots." We can usually figure these out without too much trouble, but obeying them may be another matter.

Between the "thou shalts" and the "thou shalt nots," however, are many things life brings along on which decisions have to be made. It may be that no specific *verse* gives us direction or guidance on *this* decision, so we have to look for other means.

It is a beautiful thing that God has given us *principles* to operate on in these areas, and He has implanted the Holy Spirit in our hearts to speak to us and say, "This is what I want you to do." The still small voice of the Holy Spirit of God will often guide us.

A few years ago I was in California after the Christmas holidays attending a conference in the San Francisco Bay area. After the conference I went to visit my parents in the Los Angeles area before flying back to Chicago. At the same time, another staff couple from Michigan had driven out to the conference in a Volkswagen with their six-month-old baby, Deborah. That's a long, hard trip in a VW.

After the conference was over, the couple got an idea and called me. The father said, "Hey, old buddy, what would be the possibility of you taking Deborah with you on the plane? We'll call some friends in Chicago, have them meet you at the airport and take Deborah off your hands, while we drive the Volkswagen back. That will take us about five days, and we'll pick Deborah up at our friends' home. You'll only have her for four or five hours on the plane."

From a logical standpoint, it sounded fine. Stewardesses on the plane would handle anything drastic that might come along, like changing a diaper and warming the baby's bottle. So it seemed like a very reasonable request. These were good friends of ours, so how could I possibly turn them down?

I had a couple of days before having to make the

decision, so I said, "Let me think and pray about it." I did think and pray, and as much as I wanted to say, "Yes, I'd be happy to do it," there was a feeling within me that I should say no. I had no indication from the Bible about it; it was just a feeling. In my times with the Lord, He hadn't spoken to me from some obscure passage in Ezekiel saying, "Thou shalt not take that baby on the plane [or chariot]," but there was this inner feeling of unrest and uneasiness.

The Bible says that God is not the author of confusion, but of peace (1 Corinthians 14:33). Paul also talks about the kind of decisions which often confront us (Romans 14). The particular situation he was talking about in this section was the matter of eating meat that had been offered at a pagan temple. Rather than saying it was right or wrong, Paul gave a principle and a guideline for life situations. He stated, "But he who doubts is condemned if he eats, because his eating is not from faith, and whatever is not from faith is sin" (Romans 14:23). However, Paul points out that there are some who can eat meat offered at pagan temples with a perfectly clear conscience, who have no qualms about it whatsoever, and for those it is perfectly alright to eat the meat. He goes on to say that the "eaters" and the "non-eaters" must not condemn one another. The Bible gives no room for judging another Christian's freedom or the lack of it.

Another way to look at this principle is to explain it as the "principle of peace," as Paul said, "Be anxious for nothing, but in everything by prayer and supplication with thanksgiving let your requests be made known to God. And the peace of God which surpasses all comprehension, shall guard your hearts and your minds in Christ Jesus" (Philippians 4:6-7). A long time ago I gave up trying to explain "the peace of God which surpasses all comprehension." How can you possibly explain something that you can't comprehend?

Paul also talks about the peace "ruling" in your heart (Colossians 3:15). The Greek word in this verse for *rule* means "to be the umpire of," calling an "out" or "safe" in a definite way.

In my heart, the Holy Spirit was saying about taking Deborah, "Out; don't do it"; I had doubt, unrest, and no peace about taking her on that plane.

So when her parents called, very apologetically I turned them down (because I did feel like a heel about it). I could tell by the tone of their voices on the other end of the phone that they did not completely understand my decision.

That afternoon I climbed on the airplane and flew to Chicago. We got there and the field was completely fogged in. We made three passes to try to get into O'Hare, but finally the pilot announced, "Folks, we are really sorry. We have made three attempts to land at O'Hare and we are getting low on fuel. We can't wait any longer for the ceiling to lift, so we are going to take you back to Kansas City and put you up there overnight."

I had exactly $7 in my pocket and was flying Economy. I didn't realize till that night that when you fly Economy on some airlines, they don't pay for your hotel and food if something happens. This meant that I had to find a hotel room in Kansas City for about $6.50, leaving me enough for a hot dog for supper. Thoughts of having a six-month-old baby in that hotel room, out of milk, with no clean diapers, made me break out in a cold sweat.

The Lord does want to lead us in *all* situations. I realize that the consequences don't always turn out as dramatically as mine did, and it isn't always as clear as to the *why* of His leading. But the truth is that He *wants* to lead us. If we are willing to do anything He asks of us in a given situation, if we are willing to commit it to Him in prayer and to wait on Him, He will show us His will. And we can make good decisions that are spiritual in nature and are in accordance with His plan for us.

With God's leading, a husband can make *sound and timely decisions.*

27

CHOOSING TO ENCOURAGE
by Jack

I AM convinced that there are "seasons" to all of our lives, but perhaps a woman has more definite seasons than a man. Her seasons may be divided in a number of ways, some being: "Before children," "Preschool children," "School children," and "After children."

Carole entered a different "season" just as we moved to a small townhouse in a new community and I began to travel frequently in my work. Because of a change in school systems, Lynn no longer came home for lunch.

Now my wife is not one to sit around watching TV all day, because she is an activist. Considering these circumstances, I realized that I had to start praying for Carole in a special way. I knew that probably for the first time in her life she was going to find herself with time on her hands which she would want to fill profitably. As we talked about it and prayed over the matter together, we began to ask God for areas of specific ministry and outreach.

In a few weeks, God led a young widow on the North Shore section of Chicago to begin doing Bible study with Carole. Soon Edy invited three or four of her friends to meet for Bible study and group discussion, women eager to grow in Jesus Christ. Carole and Edy began to teach them, not only how to grow in the Christian life but how to teach other women the same principles of discipleship. These women had friends who were eager to know Christ, and soon several other studies began. By the time we left the Chicago area in 1973, there were about 500 women in the north and northwest suburbs who were excited about living for Christ and studying the Bible together. These groups are being perpetuated by women in whose lives Carole and Edy had invested.

PRINCIPLE NUMBER FIVE—*Determine your wife's gifts and capabilities and encourage her accordingly.* What are your wife's gifts? Her strengths? Do you know what she enjoys and does well? Are you encouraging her along these lines to develop and use the strengths she has in whatever way God wants?

Dawson Trotman, the founder of The Navigators, used to say, "Never do anything that someone else will or can do when there is so much to be done that no one else can or will do."

Unfortunately, many men feel threatened by their wives' abilities. This attitude causes great limitations on what God wants to accomplish through that particular *couple.* God made a man and a woman to "fit together"—to complete one another—to be more effective together than either one could be alone. Some men unconsciously say, "Well, as long as my wife's gifts are mainly in the kitchen, I'll encourage her."

Now, I am glad that some of Carole's natural gifts *do* lie in the homemaking area, and that she is challenged by and enjoys our home. I have no difficulty at all delegating all responsibility in the areas of planning meals, shopping, cooking, and organizing for entertaining. I help when I can, but mainly all I am good for is walking through the kitchen. We sit down and talk about what we ought to do in the way of being hospitable and how we should entertain, but she has the gifts in that area and I am very glad to delegate it to her. Most men have no trouble with that.

But a number of men are intimidated if their wives get more phone calls than they do. And if their gifts happen to overlap, they get upset. Instead of figuring out how they as a couple can "fit together," this kind of man suddenly starts demanding so much in the home that his poor wife has no energy left to use other gifts—spiritual gifts—that God has given her with which to be creative.

God did not bring us together to compete with one another, but to complete one another. If a wife feels stifled, boxed in by being "just a housewife," if she does not feel she is living up to her God-given abilities, it may be because the husband is not following this principle to determine his wife's gifts and capabilities in all areas and encourage her accordingly.

28

CHOOSING RESPONSIBILITY
by Jack

THE TWO hardest words in the English language, or any language for that matter, for most men to say are, "I'm sorry!" Yet our last principle and guideline for being a good leader will necessitate using those two words time and again.

PRINCIPLE NUMBER SIX—*Seek responsibility and take responsibility for your actions.* Seek responsibility. Many men have abdicated their leadership and women have encouraged them to do so. Men need to take initiative in leadership. I am not talking about demanding submission; I am talking about accepting responsibility.

The second part of the guideline is just as difficult: to take responsibility for your actions. Believe it or not, but there will be times when you are 100% *wrong.* You have been the worst leader and have made the worst decisions this side of Napoleon's defeat at Waterloo. Now what are you going to do? One thing only. Say, "Honey, I'm sorry. I was wrong. Will you forgive me?" *and mean it!*

You may have to say this to your children when you have done unkind, inconsiderate, and hurtful things.

Are you man enough to say, "I'm sorry. Will you forgive me?" A good leader seeks responsibility and is willing to accept the responsibility for his actions—when they are right and when they are wrong. Especially when they are wrong.

Before we finish discussing what leadership is for a husband, we need a reminder. Submission is the life-style of *every* Christian. A Christian is, first of all, to obey God. And God says His servants are to obey their spiritual leaders, the government, their parents, their elders, and each other. That just about covers the territory! We are all called on to be "subject to one another" (Ephesians 5:21), in a context that begins the commands to husbands and wives.

Please note that the command to be "subject to one another" *precedes* the discussion on headship and submission in Ephesians 5. That is extremely significant. God did not make a mistake in putting that statement there, nor is it incompatible with what follows. As the head of my home, I have a responsibility of serving, of submitting, of looking out for Carole and Lynn with tenderness, a giving of self that must be constant. I can never, *I must never demand* submission from my wife. It is Carole's to give—or withhold. *She* is commanded in a special way to be subject to me as her husband (I'm not commanded to remind her to submit to me). If she isn't, she is disobeying God, but even then that doesn't mean that I can demand it.

In summary, then, these are the principles of good leadership:

1. Know your wife in order to look out for her welfare.

2. Keep the channels of communication open and clear. See that any generic difficulties are thought through together.

3. Set an example.

4. Make sound and timely decisions.

5. Determine your wife's gifts and capabilities and encourage her accordingly.

6. Seek responsibility and take responsibility for your actions.

Headship is leadership, a leadership of love. It is not a general commanding his army, a computer analyst pushing the right buttons, a master in charge of his slave. It is simply taking our God-given responsibility to care for our wives and families and to lead them in love toward the goals which God has chosen for us.

29

CHOOSING TO SUBMIT
by Carole

SUNLIGHT danced over the bedspread, reflected to the walls, and splashed on the blue carpet. Birds, perched on the telephone wire outside my window, competed for the cheeriest song of the day. But a greater contest was going on inside my soul and made me deaf to their music . . . a struggle which climaxed smaller battles fought during several weeks over the concept of submission.

Submission! How I hated that word. When it flashed into my mind, all I could conjure up was a nonentity, a nothing sort of yes-woman. I didn't want to be only a reflection of another person.

Yet here I was faced with the no-nonsense command of God, "Wives, be subject to your own husbands, as to the Lord" (Ephesians 5:22). I had argued with God and with everyone else that this verse could not mean what it looked like on the surface; that it was surely a cultural statement that had meaning only for Bible times.

In my stubborn resistance, I searched the Bible to see if there were exceptions to that command, examples of godly women who didn't submit to their husbands. I couldn't find any. Abigail came closest when she bypassed her drunken husband to take food to David and his men when Nabal had refused (1 Samuel 25). But she did it to save her husband and the men of his household. She was obeying the command to "do him good and not evil all the days of her life" (Proverbs 31:12).

My next attempt was to reconstruct the verse to read, "Wives, submit yourselves unto your husbands as to the Lord *when they are acting like the Lord.*" But I knew it didn't mean that.

As I searched the Word that fifth year of our marriage, I had to conclude that this verse meant I was to submit myself to Jack in the same free and "nothing-held-back" way that I wanted to submit to Jesus Christ.

Up to that point I had felt that marriage was a 50/50 proposition, and if Jack would give his 50%, I would give mine. However, it seemed that frequently we would fight to determine whose turn it was to give that 50%. I had yet to learn that a happy biblical marriage is one that is a 100% proposition with each partner willing to give 100%.

That spring, God had begun a deep work in Jack's life and I saw the need for much change in my own. I asked God to deepen me and help me grow. And one of the first seeds He planted in the soil of my mind was to "submit to your husband"—to adapt to him and let him be the leader. It was a seed I would have just as soon dumped in the "throw-away" bin.

Jack, being a strong leader of people anyway, always *had* been the head of our home and way down inside of me I knew this and respected him because of it. But it wasn't for my lack of trying to run things that he continued his leadership. I tried every wile possible to "win."

That sunny day God faced me squarely with the need

to make up my mind—was I going to obey Him or not? To obey God meant obeying Jack—when I felt like it and when I didn't feel like it; when he was loving and when he was disagreeable. It was in those "disagreeable" times that I knew I would have to do it for *God's* sake and not for *Jack's*. If Lynn didn't obey her babysitter when I had told her to, it wasn't the babysitter she was disobeying as much as me. In fact, mostly me. She might not obey for the babysitter's sake, but she needed to for my sake. The issue was clear.

God was waiting to open a closed door in my life. For me, this became a lordship decision. "If God is not Lord *of* all, He is not Lord *at* all" had been a truth I had known for years, and it was brought again to my mind. If God were not Lord of my attitudes in marriage, He was not Lord of my *life* because I was still making the decisions as to what parts of my life He could or could not control. I had to come to grips with this all-important question: was I willing to trust God in this area, *whatever it meant?* Even if it meant becoming all those things I feared most . . . a nonentity . . . a nothing? Was I willing for *God?*

Tears dropped on the pages of my Bible. After what felt like hours of inner wrestling and struggle, I finally said, "Yes, Lord. Whatever it means, I really want to submit to Jack because *You* say to, and I want to obey."

At the moment I took that step of submitting my will, I could not see how it would turn out well. I honestly thought Jack might become selfish, demanding, and unfair. But the *exact opposite* happened. When Jack found out that I wasn't fighting to get my own way or to run his life, or to change him, he became more unselfish, more tender, less demanding. He asked my opinion on things he had never asked before. We grew closer as he included me in a greater variety of decisions. Something beautiful happened in our lives.

And instead of deteriorating into a blob, I felt like I was emerging from a cocoon to stretch my wings and fly . . . and find out who I really was.

Now please don't think that I've "arrived," for I have a long way to go. I have an independent streak in me you wouldn't believe. It still makes me want things *my* way in *my* time with *my* needs paramount. Self continues to demand, "Meet my needs." But love, God's love within me, cries, "Let me meet *your* needs."

Most of us don't want men we can dominate, but many of us will try our best to get our own way. So if we can't dominate, we will maneuver. Now I am a pretty good maneuverer, but God showed me that was wrong too. To manipulate, to control, to manage are all verbs expressing the same power play.

I guess the most exciting thing I discovered was that "God's commandments are not grievous" (1 John 5:3, KJV). In other words, His commands are not to make us unhappy or to be hard on us, but to make us live life freely, fully, and joyfully.

I have been reading a number of women authors who feel that anyone who is in submission to another individual is inferior, which, if logically carried through, would mean that children are inferior to parents, younger people are inferior to older people, we are inferior to our government, and, most of all, that Christ was inferior to the Father because Jesus submitted Himself to God the Father. The latter is heresy, the former foolish.

Most of these women have decided that submission is out of date, or a result of the fall, or a statement that Paul made in the flesh before he was enlightened. Interestingly, I have never read in any of these books the thought that the husband's command to "love his wife as his own body," which is in the same paragraph, is anything but literal and for our day.

We must stop buying what the world is trying to sell. It will lead to heartbreak and sorrow if we pursue it.

The other extreme is to put a straight jacket on wives by binding them with the few short passages directed specifically to wives. *All* of Scripture is for wives. All of the Bible is for every Christian. Scriptures such as "speak the truth in love" and "admonish one another daily" are totally compatible with being a wife who is in submission to her husband (see Ephesians 4:15; Romans 15:14).

Submission is an attitude of *heart* . . . and an attitude of yieldedness and of love. In our family it works like this: in every decision, major or minor, I freely and openly tell Jack my opinions and feelings. If we don't agree, we come to a compromise solution 99% of the time. (This is not like the couple where the wife wanted a fur coat and the husband wanted a new car, so they compromised; she bought the coat, but kept it in the garage.) In a small number of cases when we can't come to a compromise, it is Jack's responsibility before God to make the final decision.

In some instances Jack decides *my* way because he loves me. If we have diametrically opposed views on a couch, for instance, and can't find one we both really like (which has never been the case, incidentally), Jack may buy the one I like because I have to live with it more hours of the day than he does.

However, after a full discussion of a matter if he feels before God that we must go in one direction while I feel we should go in the other, it is Jack's responsibility to make that decision. And it is my responsibility to submit to his decision . . . and get behind him in it too. God will hold the husband responsible for the decision, but he holds the wife responsible for her submission to that decision.

As I think about it, I am aware that most women do not have a problem with their husbands making the final decision if they feel that they have been truly *heard* and their viewpoint *understood.* Men, please take special note of that last sentence. Some husbands don't give their wives the opportunity to interact, to express all of their thoughts and feelings, and to be *valued* in those opinions. When a woman does not feel her viewpoint has been completely listened to, it is difficult for her not to be resentful when her husband makes a decision in which they are not in agreement. Of course, even in this a wife has no excuse for a bitter and resentful heart. God *is* in control and He will give grace to be rid of bitterness if we ask Him (Hebrews 12:15).

Wives have said to me, "If my husband would fulfill his part—to love me as Christ loves the church—I would be more than willing to submit to him."

Of course. Then it would be so easy. But there is no verse which reads, "*If* the husband acts lovingly, then a wife should submit to him." Neither is there a verse which reads, "If a wife submits to her husband, then he should act lovingly." This is not a "I-will-if-you-will" situation. A husband is commanded to love his wife as Christ loved the church if she *never* submits to him. A wife is commanded to submit to her husband *regardless* of his demonstrating love for her. It is only in the 100% commitment to the command of God and to our mates that we are able to have harmony and peace in our marriages.

Is there no recourse? Yes, there is.

The best advice I was ever given was a few months after I determined to obey this command to submit. At a conference in Colorado, a wife said, "Whenever my husband makes a wrong decision, or does something I don't like, or whenever I see a characteristic in his life that is ugly, I do one thing." I was literally sitting on the edge of my chair in anticipation. *At last* I was about to learn a tremendous tool to use to change my husband, and I was all ears.

She continued, "I pray!"

I felt like someone had stuck a finger in the rising dough of my expectations and it had fallen with a thud. I thought, *Now come on, friend. You just* have *to do more than that.* My philosophy at that time was "faith without hints is dead."

But as she continued, my hopes began to rise again.

She said, "Inevitably when I pray, one of three things happens. First, my husband changes. God *is* in the business of changing people. [I since have learned to keep a separate prayer list just for Jack—one he never sees. It has been exciting over the years to see the way God has answered requests on that list.]

"Second, my husband asks me about the decision or problem again. I have had a chance to pray about it, think through on it, and perhaps find how to approach it in another way. God has put it in his heart to ask me again and has prepared his heart for my answer. He accepts it in a positive way and change occurs.

"Third, God lays it on my heart to bring the matter up again and share my thoughts freely. We are *one*. There is nothing that should come between us. God gives me the wisdom in sharing this in a positive, constructive way instead of negatively, and he accepts it."

As I began to practice her advice, I was astounded. It really worked. I found that as I prayed over the difficulties, God erased some of them completely from my heart. It was as though He said, "I'll take care of that. Leave it to Me. You won't even have to bring it up." And I could forget it. At other times, as I would pray, the worry would be wiped away, but the hard little knot of coldness remained. This became my way of knowing it was a matter I needed to bring up again at the first available opportunity. But I still had had a chance to pray and think about it, so it wasn't expressed in anger.

After a time, I added a *fourth* point to her list. In the area of decisionmaking, at least in our home, Jack is generally right. When I am able to be objective about it, I see it. So, in these cases of disagreement, God changes *my* heart as I pray. He has saved us from a big scene and I am grateful for that.

God is helping me grow in practicing this plan, though I fail frequently. I erupt instead of praying. I have discovered that it does work, however, and not just with my husband. I have a feeling that Jack practices it with *me* too, which is a mighty good idea. Husbands can't change wives. They may be able to control them to some degree, but they can't change them. Only God can do that.

I think of this poem frequently in relation to learning submission:

> *Lord, I am learning*
>
> *That marriage from first to last*
> *Is an adventure—*
> *A long series of recurring "happenings"*
> *In which we triumph or fail.*

That when I let God be God
When according to Your Word
I joyfully submit
To my husband's authority
My sense of fulfillment
Is at high peak.

I can face life head-on
I can live with myself creatively—
Not ironclad rules
But ironclad love.
It works, Lord
Just as You said it would.

I am learning.[1]

NOTES: 1. Ruth Harms Calkin, "I Am Learning," *Tell Me Again,*
         Lord, I Forget (Elgin, Illinois: David C. Cook Publishing
         Co., 1974), pages 22-23.

The Physical Relationship

30

CHOOSING TO BE "ONE FLESH"
by Jack

M Y WIFE calls it "the oil in the machinery." To me, it
is the "frosting on the cake." And there is no mas-
culine/feminine contradiction.

It can be the greatest fun in all of life or more trouble
and heartache than anything else in the marriage relationship. It has many names, some beautiful, some
coarse. The simplest name is *sex*.

When God created man and woman, He made them
male and female. As God looked out over His creation,
He said, "Behold, it is *very* good" (Genesis 1:31). In His
wonderful wisdom God designed sexual intercourse for
at least three reasons: for the propagation of the human
race, for the expression of the kind of love between a
man and wife which nourishes true oneness, and for
pleasure.

Some today have become trapped in the snares of the
so-called "new morality" (which really is the old im-
morality with a new name) or in situation ethics. Some
have bought what the world is selling in the Playboy
Philosophy. Others, reacting violently to these philos-
ophies, have landed back among the distorted images of
somber, negative Puritanism.

But according to the Bible, sex is a gift from God with a wonderful purpose. The first two purposes mentioned—for the propagation of the human race and for the building of love—are generally accepted by the Christian world. Scripture passages such as Genesis 1:27-28, 9:1, and Psalm 127:3 both command and bless the propagating of the human race. God could have invented other ways for us to conceive children. He could have had us exchange ear wax with Q-tips. It is beautiful to me that God came up with a way of promoting the human race that was so irresistible that men and women can't stay away from it. God had a great idea when He invented something so unique and delightful that the growth of the human race was insured.

The second purpose—to promote mutual love—is shown us in the phrase "and the two shall become one flesh." This statement, found four times in Scripture (Genesis 2:24; Matthew 19:5; Mark 10:7; Ephesians 5:31), certainly has in it the aspects of emotional, spiritual, and mental oneness. But the ultimate meaning here is physical—a blending of two bodies into one flesh to promote mutual love.

Some people have more difficulty accepting the third purpose for sex, which is that it is for our enjoyment. It was given us for pure pleasure. The Scriptures which make this fact clear are often overlooked. Paul said, "But because of immoralities, let each man have his own wife, and let each woman have her own husband" (1 Corinthians 7:2). The pull of the sex drive is so great, Paul gives a warning about it to those who are unmarried and then says, "Let the husband fulfill his duty to his wife, and likewise also the wife to her husband" (7:3). The revised version translates *duty* as "conjugal rights." Now the expression *conjugal rights* or *duty* doesn't communicate too well to me, but what this really means is that we are not to withhold the *pleasure* that is rightfully owed each other; we are to enjoy one another.

Sex is a God-given drive. Every God-given drive has a design in which it is to operate. For instance, hunger is a drive given to us by God. He knew that He had to do something to insure that we eat in order to keep us alive to propagate the human race, because dead people do not reproduce. Unless there was some mechanism in us that would indicate to us, "It's time to eat; I'm hungry," some of us might starve to death. Some would be so busy, they would forget to eat entirely. (For others of us, we'd like to turn that drive off for awhile so we wouldn't fight a continual "battle of the bulge.") The hunger drive is given by God, but the Scriptures are clear that this drive is to be handled within the framework or design of moderation.

Ambition is a God-given drive also, but it is to be handled within the design of God's will. As long as we are in God's will in our jobs or in other situations and walking daily in the light of His will, there is absolutely nothing wrong with godly ambition, initiative, and creativity.

In the same way, sex is a God-given drive, designed by God to operate within the framework of marriage. Within this framework, it produces harmony, happiness, and freedom. Those who misuse this gift apart from God's design find heartache, shallowness, and anxiety. The Playboy Philosophy of "using" a woman for a plaything to gratify the desires of the flesh is diametrically opposed to God's design and program for sex.

I am emphasizing the pleasure aspect of sex because many still have problems believing God chose to delight us with this gift. Within His framework and design, sex has been given to us to enjoy. Hang-ups from our backgrounds making us feel that sex is dirty, sinful, or shameful have devastating effects on us and on our children when in turn they marry.

A beautiful illustration of the pleasure of sex may be found in the life of one of the great patriarchs of the faith. God had promised Abraham a son whose descendants would become as the sands on the seashore and the stars of heaven. But no son was born to Abraham and Sarah, and he was now 100 years old and his wife 90. That seems to be pretty old for much of anything. But Abraham continued to depend on God to fulfill His promise to him and Sarah.

Finally, God sent three angels to Abraham and speaking through them said, "Where is Sarah, your wife?"

Abraham answered, "Behold, in the tent."

Then God said, "I will surely return to you at this time next year, and behold, Sarah your wife shall have a son."

"And Sarah was listening at the tent door, which was behind him. Now Abraham and Sarah were old, advanced in age; it had ceased to be with Sarah after the manner of women" (Genesis 18:9-11).

The last phrase, "it had ceased to be with Sarah after the manner of women," could mean a number of things, but the foremost meaning undoubtedly is that she could no longer conceive. A secondary meaning could be that she was no longer enjoying her husband physically.

"And Sarah laughed to herself, saying, 'After I have become old, shall I have *pleasure*, my lord being old also?'" (18:12)

Isn't it interesting that the Spirit of God chose this word to use here? "Shall I have *pleasure*?" (This is the same Hebrew word that is used for Eden, as in "the

Garden of *Eden*.") From the response of God in the next statement, we know that Sarah also meant the pleasure of having a son, but I really think something else was on her mind as well. It was not unusual for men of Abraham's age to father many children; indeed, he had fathered Ishmael by Hagar some years before and would have other children by Keturah after Sarah's death. Yet Sarah here mentions Abraham's age as well as her own in the sentence about having pleasure. This makes me feel that they probably weren't enjoying each other physically at that time.

They then had "pleasure," and it produced the joy of a son from their union. Isaac was born and, many years later, married Rebekah.

> So Isaac lived in Gerar. When the men of the place asked about his wife, he said, "She is my sister," for he was afraid to say, "My wife," thinking, "The men of the place might kill me on account of Rebekah, for she is beautiful." And it came about, when he had been there a long time, that Abimelech king of the Philistines looked out through a window and saw, and behold, Isaac was caressing his wife Rebekah (Genesis 26:6-8).

One translation says, "Sporting with" (KJV). You may be sure they were not playing chess. "Then Abimelech called Isaac and said, 'Behold, certainly she is your wife! How then did you say, "She is my sister"?' And Isaac said to him, 'Because I said, "Lest I die on account of her" ' " (Genesis 26:9).

Apparently Isaac was doing something with Rebekah that he would not do with his sister. Whatever it was, caressing, fondling, "sporting with," you may be sure they were delighting in one another.

The whole book of the Song of Solomon is a love poem between two people who are in love with one another. The Bible uses very intimate and beautiful language to describe the relationship these two lovers had (see 1:13; 4:5, 10; 5:4, 16).

If we have background cobwebs remaining in our minds, let us ask God for the clean purifying sweep of His Word, that we may know that not only is sex within marriage straight from the hand of God, but He gave it to us as a gift to *enjoy*.

31

CHOOSING TO UNDERSTAND SEXUAL DIFFERENCES
by Jack

SEXUALLY, men and women are different. And anatomy is only a small part of that difference. We are diverse in our approaches, our responses, and what it means to us. Unless we understand and adjust to these variances, we are in trouble.

Here are some distinctives:

• To a man sex is a delightful intermission in the drama; to a woman it is inexorably woven into the fabric of the whole.

• The male sex drive is generated by physical needs, accompanied by emotional needs; a woman's drive stems from emotional needs, along with physical needs.

• A man thinks, *How often?* A woman ponders, *How?*

• A man's thought is reduced to the moment; a woman's to what is *produced* by the moment. (During intercourse, a man rarely thinks of the act resulting in a baby, while this may be much on a woman's mind.)

• A man is quick to react to stimulation; a woman, comparatively slow to react, needs to be stimulated.

• A man is primarily stimulated by *one* of his senses—sight; a woman is stimulated by all five plus one—touch, hearing, sight, taste, smell, and the extra one of *tenderness*. (This difference is an important one to remember as a number of wives have confided to Carole and me that they were unable to respond physically to their husbands because they smelled. Perspiration, stale smoke, and bad breath can all inhibit a woman's enjoyment of sex. This is also true of men, of course; they can be turned off by unpleasant smells, but women seem to be more careful about such things.)

To summarize with an illustration: A man is like an electric light bulb—you flip a switch and on he goes. A woman is more like an electric iron—you flip a switch and it takes a little time to warm up. When you turn it off, it takes a bit of time to cool off too.

Now if you don't remember any of the other differences, please remember that one. It is very important in learning to be a lover. And men need to learn to be lovers if they are to satisfy the needs of their wives.

I get discouraged sometimes when I talk with some men about their pattern in making love. Some have the lovemaking instincts of a frog, and maybe I'm being disrespectful to a frog!

Note this often typical situation. He gets home from work and gives her a little peck on the cheek. They have supper. He sits down and relaxes, reads the paper, watches some TV, then it is bedtime. So he goes into the bathroom, does his little chores, and gets into his pajamas. She does the same thing and they climb in bed. They read a little while, perhaps, then she reaches over and turns off her light. He reads a few minutes longer, and finally reaches over and turns off his light. All is quiet.

And then, suddenly, out of the dark . . .

comes a hand.

What a romantic setting! What psychological build-up! What creative imagination! Like I said, "All the instincts of a frog!"

Now, men we can do better than that.

One time, a month after we had presented this subject to a group at a seminar, I ran into one of the women who had attended. She smiled and said, "You know, now my husband on occasion will call in the afternoon from the office and as we are chatting will say, 'By the way, honey, will you please turn on the iron.' "

She was excited about that.

If a man has a desire to make love that evening and has it on his mind all day just waiting to get home that night, but his wife doesn't know anything about it, and he pulls that "hand in the dark" routine, if she can respond with enthusiasm, then he has a very unusual wife.

On the other hand, if as he leaves the house in the morning, he gives her a very warm kiss and communicates in their own secret little code that he is looking forward to some fun that night, it will turn up her thermostat just a bit and it will stay warm all day long. By the time he gets home, the atmosphere has already been created and the two are far more likely to have a wonderful time that night.

Now what I have written may not apply to everyone of you. We are all unique individuals. But *think*, then *talk* together about your needs and ideas to promote greater mutual enjoyment in your sex lives. If you want an "angel in the home and a tigress in bed," you must communicate what excites and pleasures you.

Have you ever discussed the degree of dress or undress which stimulate desire? Or the kind of apparel? Some men actually don't like black nightgowns. But their wives have been buying black nightgowns for years with the mistaken notion that their husbands found them sexy.

Those of us who have been married some years hopefully have gotten courageous enough to walk into the lingerie department of a large store and bravely walk up to the counter (as though we do it every day of the week) and say, "I'll take one of *those*." The "those" is something that she will wear only for you, a gesture of love and appreciation, but also something that will excite you.

May God deliver us from the "hand in the dark" approach. We need to use our imaginations and our creativity to set the mood for our lovemaking. Sex should be fun. And variety will enhance that fun.

Have you ever used your imagination to create a whole other world for your lovemaking? Your imagination can transport you out of that bedroom and the monotony of its four walls, so that you can journey together to a desert island where you are marooned with no rescue in sight, or a little cabin, snowbound after skiing all day. Imagining wholesome situations, various times, diverse places, all can add to your enjoyment together.

Good ideas can also be obtained from many marriage manuals, but many couples read the wrong ones or too many of them. They get so wrapped up in the "ideal," that they become totally unreal. Many manuals, for instance, hold that the epitome of the sex relationship is to have a climax together. This can be like a carrot held out to a bunch of racing rabbits—always just out of reach. As long as both are enjoying the physical relationship and both are usually *reaching* a climax, it just isn't that important to reach it together. The enjoyment is the primary concern. And the climax will not be the same every time. I have talked to people who think that unless they have the greatest, most exciting feeling in their lives each time, they are disappointed. It *is* always exciting—or should be. It *is* always thrilling, but it is *never* the same.

One of my favorite meals is a steak, baked potato, rolls, and apple pie. That is a real banquet for me. But I also like McDonald's hamburgers. In fact, I'm crazy about McDonald's hamburgers. And I am satisfied with either the steak dinner or a McDonald's hamburger.

That is sort of the way it is with sex. Sometimes it's like the steak, baked potato, rolls, and apple pie. At other times, it's just like McDonald's hamburgers. But it is always great. And it satisfies my needs and hers.

I hope you are reading this aloud and together as a couple. And that this will cause you to stop and talk about the whole area of the physical union, which is probably the most neglected area of communication between husbands and wives. It needs to be talked about at length, prayed over, and experienced together so that in a more full way each year, the two of you will truly become "one flesh."

32

CHOOSING THE BEST
by Carole

WE DROVE along in silence for several miles. I could tell by the minuscule frown on her face that she was thinking deeply. The conversation had turned to marriage and it was obvious that this wife of several years had a problem. As we left the city and the traffic thinned, she took a deep breath and said, "But how can I really keep my marriage *exciting?* Ours is a good marriage. We love each other. But somehow the fun, excitement, and sparkle have faded from our relationship. Is it possible to *really* keep the excitement in a marriage?"

As we talked, it became apparent that she had stopped doing a great many little things she had done at first. She didn't greet her husband at the door any more with a smile and a kiss; she and her husband had stopped dating when the children came; someone else now took him to the airport for his trips and picked him up. But mainly it was their sex life that had become routine and dull. When the *fun* of sex evaporated into monotony, the little private jokes between them disappeared, and the electricity generated by both was cut off and no "sparks" remained. Exit excitement.

A unique, exciting physical relationship does not just happen. As in other areas of our marriages, it has to be worked at and planned for.

A woman has a difficult time separating love and sex. They are intertwined clear down to her inner being. At times a woman longs much more for the closeness and intimacy of the sex act than she does for the thrill of it. Most women long to be *held*, totally apart from sex. Understanding husbands need to be aware of the need for closeness that many wives have.

God has depths in the sexual area of our lives that few of us will ever plumb. It is difficult sometimes to keep God's perspective in a world that tries continually to make sex into one of the better body functions. One article to college students pointed out that it shouldn't hurt any more to break up after a fellow and girl had slept together than if they hadn't had intercourse. After all, the article said, it is just another body function. How sad! The shallowness of this point of view is leaving frustrated and despairing people in its wake.

God's plan is for sex to be like a deep, refreshing well, with water that keeps springing up—invigorating, refreshing, pure. Solomon teaches us that when we make God's gift of sex impure, in other words, when we commit adultery and fornication, it is like stagnant, shallow water on the streets of our lives (see Proverbs 5:15-19).

Do we want the "muddy puddles" of casual sex or the "deep wells" which exist within the marriage relationship? We can't have it both ways. And the choice is ours. God will give us the deep wells to refresh our spirits and our bodies, wells that can be more beautiful with passing years. God wants a *growing* depth in our relation together, and this is a "bottomless" well as far as I am concerned. One that can keep being explored with depths never reached. It has been said, "Sex is not something you do. Sex is something you are *becoming* together." And this is true.

Sex never needs to be boring or routine. God created us with a desire which is much like taking a long, cold drink of water on a hot summer afternoon. "Let your fountain be blessed, and rejoice in the wife of your youth. As a loving hind and a graceful doe, let her breasts satisfy you at all times; be exhilarated always with her love" (Proverbs 5:18-19).

Our God is a creative God. He can give us creative ideas in our sex lives. Do you ever pray for creativity from God in this area? You may. Do you ever pray that you will be a blessing to your mate in your physical relationship? You may. Do you ever ask God for His point of view when you experience hang-ups from your childhood? Do. God is interested in *all* our problems including those we may have in this area.

One Old Testament word for intercourse is *to know*. "Adam *knew* Eve his wife, and she conceived" (Genesis 4:1, 25, KJV). This is a beautiful word because, to me, sex is total communication—body, soul, spirit ˥otal knowledge completes communication.

That's what it should be, but often isn't.

Probably one of the first things a couple needs to do is to *know and understand the facts*. Many people have a terrible time just speaking out loud the correct name for parts of the body. Then they wonder why it is difficult for them to communicate about intimate areas of sex.

So, if you have never done it before, read a good marriage manual on sex *aloud and together*. Herbert Miles' *Sexual Happiness in Marriage*, Tim and Beverly LaHaye's *The Act of Marriage*, and Ed and Gaye Wheat's

Intended for Pleasure are excellent and from a Christian point of view. Or listen to Dr. Ed Wheat's tapes together to get a medical doctor's perspective (see *Recommended Reading* on these books and tapes).

Engaged couples should be encouraged to read these books separately during the engagement period, and then aloud together a week or so before they are married. If they do this, it will enable them to begin to communicate in an area where so many can't get the words past their throats.

It is hard to believe that in this day of sex instruction in schools, on TV and in the movies, sex is *still* the number one matter couples have trouble talking about. Free and open discussion is essential. It is the first step forward on the road called "Excitement."

33

CHOOSING TO GIVE
by Carole

ONE summer four women came to me within a week with problems that I thought were unusual at the time, but now know to be quite common. As they shared their experiences, I discovered that God had foreseen the difficulties and written down the answers many years ago. The Bible is the best marriage manual in existence and it has many practical answers to sexual problems. It shouldn't surprise us that the inventor of marriage knows how to handle the difficulties, but sometimes the Bible is the last place we look for solutions.

The first woman had been married a number of years, but had never experienced a climax. The second was married to a man who so repulsed her, she couldn't stand to have him come near her. The third, a young woman married for two years, was so shy that she was afraid of undressing in the same room with her husband. And the fourth woman said that her husband hadn't come *near her* in four years (this was not a case of impotency due to alcohol or to some other physical problem).

The solution to all four problems is condensed into

one word—*obedience*. Obedience, not to husband or to wife, but to God Himself.

Does that sound too simple? Oh, that it were! The two things that are necessary are having God's perspective on the whole idea of sex and being committed to obeying God in that perspective.

Remember, while God doesn't give us chapters of the Bible detailing answers to sexual problems, He does give us commands that insure a healthy, beautiful physical relationship. And when He gives a command, He *will* give the wisdom, insight, and strength to us to obey that command if we are *willing* to do so. God's principles are found in a part of Paul's first letter to the Corinthians:

> The husband should give his wife what is due to her as his wife, and the wife should be as fair to her husband. The wife has no longer full rights over her own person, but shares them with her husband. In the same way the husband shares his personal rights with his wife. Do not cheat each other of normal sexual intercourse, unless of course you both decide to abstain temporarily to make special opportunity for prayer. But afterwards you should resume relations as before, or you will expose yourselves to the obvious temptation of Satan (1 Corinthians 7:3-8, PH).

Does that teaching still sound too simple? Oh that we could *really* have God's perspective on our physical problems. That we could understand how a great many of our sexual difficulties are because we are selfish . . . we want to *get* instead of *giving*.

Notice how specifically God's principles from this passage answer the problems of the four wives which I listed earlier.

GOD'S VIEWPOINT AND COMMAND:	ANSWER TO:
"Do not cheat each other of normal sexual intercourse."	The wife who never had experienced orgasm *is* being cheated of normal sexual intercourse and needs to ask God for a wise counselor to help find the reason.
Neither husband nor wife have "full rights" over their own persons, but share them. Their bodies belong to each other. Before God, they are one and unashamed.	The wife repulsed by her husband—how can she be repulsed by a part of herself?
	The wife afraid to undress in the same room with her husband.
The husband and wife are not to withhold intercourse from each other.	The husband who hadn't come near his wife in four years. His sin is against God as well as against his wife.

God *will* enable and help us figure out the answers to the "why" and "what-to-do-about-it" questions. We need to do two things. First, pray, and then communicate to our mates about our problems. I am not suggesting that the wife whose husband repulses her say, "Hey, you are repulsive to me. I can't stand your touch." (She would never have to be repulsed again, but she wouldn't have a husband either.) But she may need to say, "You know, I am not responding to you physically in the way that I know you want me to and the way I want to. Let's talk about it and pray about it together."

The paragraph in 1 Corinthians not only has the generic solution to the problems of these four wives, but it has many other suggestions for us to consider. Paul says that we are not to withhold sex from one another or we may expose ourselves to temptation (7:5). If we couple this with the words of Jesus, "It is inevitable that stumbling blocks come; but woe to that man through whom the stumbling block [temptation] comes" (Matthew 18:7), we see some significant truth. Wives . . . and husbands . . . are no doubt the single greatest cause of temptation for their partners. And many are not even aware of it. God says you are absolutely wrong to punish your husband or your wife by withholding yourself from your mate sexually. This can cause problems of temptation and the Bible says woe to *you* if you are the cause. God calls it sin.

Wives seem to have a special problem with this withholding, perhaps unconsciously. If a husband has been grouchy all day, snapping at his wife and children, blaming her for the flat tire he had, his hard day at the office, and his upset stomach, and then wants to make love at bedtime, his wife suddenly develops a splitting headache.

Now maybe she really *does* have a headache as a result of the miserable day. At other times, however, the headache is a conscious or unconscious rejection—a punishment for his ill treatment of her.

Love and sex are intertwined in the make-up of a woman. It is sometimes impossible to "turn on" physically at night if conflicts have not been resolved. Yes, impossible! Well, impossible for a woman, but *not for*

God. The Bible says, "With God *all* things are possible" (Matthew 19:26).

From a man's vantage point, he must understand that a wife desperately needs tenderness, understanding, and love. To give herself freely to him, she needs to talk about those conflicts and have them solved *before* making love. But a wife has to realize, too, that even when her husband is ugly and unloving and the problem is still unresolved, it is wrong for her to strike back by withholding her love sexually.

Unless both are willing to give even when they don't feel like giving, friction will result. Let's suppose that within the first year or two of marriage, a couple has developed a good sex life together.

A marriage relationship with a happy sex life might diagram something like this:

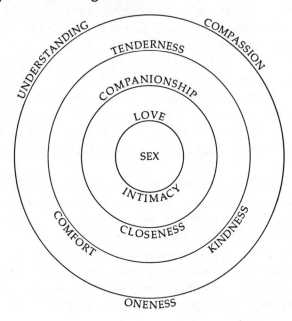

If the sex life of a married couple is happy, it is a small fraction of the total relationship—perhaps 5%. But if it is unhappy, it colors everything else and becomes closer to 90% of the relationship because it affects many other parts of life.

Let's develop the illustration of a couple with an unhappy sex life further.

One month the husband changes jobs, his new boss starts criticizing his work, his nerves get on edge, and he comes home irritable and unhappy. In fact, he's downright belligerent and takes his frustrations out on his wife. That night he really needs comfort and consolation and so that hand reaches out in the dark—he wants her.

But she can't . . . or won't . . . respond. She murmurs, "Not tonight."

Now this strikes at the very heart of his person, which is where she meant for it to strike. He has hurt her and she is hitting back.

Now what happens?

The next day, his attitude is ugly at work and terrible at home. Things go from bad to worse. He wants to make love again that night, but this time his wife turns him down with vehemence.

So the day after that the husband is so low that he has to reach up to touch bottom. And so the vicious cycle continues downward.

If a divorce occurs, the sex life (or lack of it) may get blamed. But actually the primary cause in this case was allowing bad attitudes to *affect* the sex life. These attitudes "strip the gears" in people's lives. This is why I like to call sex the "oil in the machinery."

The building up of problems, such as the ones just described, would make the relationship diagram look something like this:

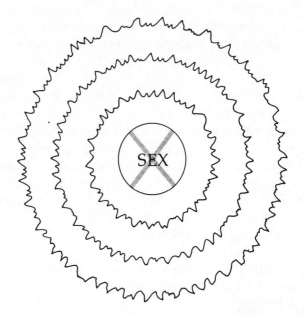

However, if a wife can say in response to her husband's desire (even when he has been a bear all day), "Lord, You know how hard it is for me to respond . . . or even want to respond to him. He has been just awful all day. I am having a hard time forgiving him, let alone forgetting and responding to him. But for You, Lord, and for our love and marriage, I want to be able to respond in love. Help me." God will help.

And in responding with love, the oil in the machinery of life will smooth out his worries and bind his hurts. Your "feast of love" may result in an opportunity to talk out the frustrations resulting in a smoothing out of the marriage relationship and a deeper, more loving oneness will result.

This would make the relationship diagram look something like this:

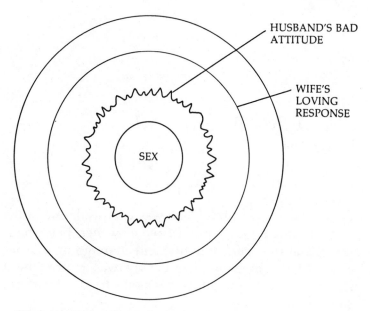

We can never build a happy marriage on resentful attitudes. It will take a miracle touch from God to turn a bitter attitude to one of forgiveness and love. But our God is a miracle-working God, and His power can create a new attitude in our hearts, if we will but ask Him for it.

34

CHOOSING TO EXPLORE
by Carole

SHE wasn't just pretty, she was beautiful, one of the most attractive women I have ever met: black hair, lovely features, perfect figure, and an outgoing personality. At the moment, her beauty was marred by a slightly red nose and puffy eyes as she tried to relate her story to me.

"Several years ago I heard you talk on how important it is for wives to let their husbands know they are wanted," she began, "but I didn't listen. I had never turned my husband down when he wanted to make love, but I was never all that eager for it either. However, we had a good marriage and I thought we were quite happy. Then my world collapsed. He had an affair with a woman at work—a woman who isn't even pretty. But she let him know that she was attracted to him and *wanted* him, and he couldn't resist her."

She twisted her handkerchief into a tiny ball and dabbed at her eyes. "Please feel free to tell my story," she continued. "I don't want anyone to go through the hell that I've known. I know now that husbands *need* to be wanted."

Her husband was a Christian, though not a strong

one. What he had done was sin . . . against the Lord and against his wife. If he had asked, God would have given him the strength to resist this temptation and to take the "way of escape" which is promised for every testing (1 Corinthians 10:13). But this wife knew that part of the blame was hers as well. Her husband had a need which she was not fulfilling, and while she had learned of that need in time to save her marriage, heartache and scars remained.

The Book of Proverbs describes a godly wife like this: "The heart of her husband doth safely trust in her, so that he shall have no need of spoil" (Proverbs 31:11, KJV). The spoil from war often consisted of riches and women slaves. I wonder if this is saying that a godly wife so satisfies her husband's needs that he has no longing for the power of wealth and desire for other women. *The Living Bible* paraphrases that verse, "She will richly satisfy his needs."

An article Jack and I read early in our marriage stated that most men actually want three different functions from the women they marry. They want a wife, a mother, and an exciting companion in bed. (This article said a "mistress," but that could be misunderstood. Jack says "tigress," and perhaps that communicates much better.)

With God's help, a woman can be all three.

When a man is sick, hurt, defeated, he needs the mother-type—to comfort, tend his hurts, and nurse his ills. Most of the time he needs a wife who is a companion, friend, idea-bouncer, encourager, helpmeet. In bed, he wants a creative woman, who is fun and who wants *him*.

A few men may be threatened if a wife takes an aggressive role and this whole area needs to be talked about together. But the vast majority of men want a woman to need them . . . to really want them sexually.

The man needs to know he is important enough to be desired, wonderful enough to be exciting, able enough to bring a woman to heights no one else can. It is up to the wife to convince her husband that he is of inestimable value both as a lover and as a *man* . . . to reach out to him and let him know how great is her love and desire for him.

Way down in the depths of a man's soul lies a longing . . . a longing to be wanted . . .a *need* to be wanted. A loving wife will see that need and meet it with joy.

SECTION VII

Conclusion

Conclusion

35

CHOOSING MARRIAGE
by Carole

THE package was on the dining room table when I walked in the door. I stared at it blankly for a full minute before the pieces fit as to how it got there and who had sent it. Then I sat down and cried for five minutes. Tears of joy and thanksgiving.

Jack was overseas . . . an extended trip which made it impossible for him to be home on our 27th wedding anniversary. We hadn't discussed it a great deal, but it was understood that we would celebrate on his return. But there, resplendent in white paper and giant bow, was a gift from him accompanied by a love-filled card written before he left.

He had secretly arranged with a friend, who had a key to our house, to surprise me on our anniversary. After I stopped crying, I opened the package to find a beautiful travel bag—Jack's way of saying, "I hope you can go with me next time."

Jack has grown increasingly more thoughtful over the years. I spent the next hour staring out into the sunshine mulling over memories of past anniversaries.

Oh, that marriage was always like that!

Shortly before the trip, I had rushed into the house

after a fast game of tennis all warm and perspiry, make-up completely gone. Jack had been working at home all morning and was in a hurry to get back to the office, so I paused to fix him lunch before getting cleaned up. As I kissed him goodbye, I said, "I promise to look better when you get home."

He answered absently, "Why, are you going to get your hair done this afternoon?"

I howled. "I've just *had* my hair done . . . yesterday," I replied.

He looked sheepish, grinned weakly, and hastily retreated.

Marriages are made of such happenings. The beautiful, the irritating, the routine, the humorous, the difficult, the dramatic.

Marriage is an enormous enigma, a colossal conundrum. It is agonizing adjusting, pain and pleasure, delight and demands. It is a mixture of the mundane, the ecstatic, the commonplace, the romantic. It comes in waves, ripples, bubbles, and splashes. Its days contain thunder, sunlight, hail, wind, rain. Its hues are the rainbow's spectrum, but prominent are shades of red, purple, yellow, and gray. It is intimacy, distance, closeness, awayness. It is a quiet melody, an earthy novel, an obscure mystery, the greatest show on earth.

It is choices. Choosing to love, to understand, to enjoy, to know. It is choosing . . . marriage.

To this we attest. It is so much more fun living it than writing about it! So we are done with the writing.

RECOMMENDED READING

MARRIAGE

Fritze, J. A. *The Essence of Marriage*. Grand Rapids, Michigan: Zondervan Publishing House, 1969.
The chapters on differences between men and women and the art of communication are excellent.

LaHaye, Tim. *How to Be Happy Though Married*. Wheaton, Illinois: Tyndale House Publishers, 1968.

Rice, Shirley. *The Christian Home*. The Tabernacle Church of Norfolk, 7120 Granby Street, Norfolk, Virginia, 1965.

Shedd, Charlie W. *Letters to Karen*. Nashville, Tennessee: Abingdon Press, 1965.
The book is for engaged or married women.

Shedd, Charlie W. *Letters to Philip*. Garden City, New York: Doubleday & Company, Inc., 1968.
The book is for engaged or married men.

Timmons, Tim. *Maximum Marriage*. Old Tappan, New Jersey: Fleming H. Revell Company, 1976.

Trobisch, Walter. *I Married You*. New York: Harper & Row, Publishers, 1971.
The book is excellent for counseling engaged couples and for marrieds.

COMMUNICATION

Augsburger, David W. *Caring Enough to Confront*. Glendale, California: Regal Books, 1973.

Shedd, Charlie W. *Talk to Me*. New York: Pillar Books, 1976.

Small, Dwight Hervey. *After We've Said "I Do."* Old Tappan, New Jersey: Fleming H. Revell Company, 1968.

The book contains some good material on communication, presented in a thesis-like approach.

Wright, H. Norman. *Communication: Key to Your Marriage*. Glendale, California: Regal Books, 1974.

DIFFERENCES BETWEEN MEN AND WOMEN

Osborne, Cecil. *The Art of Understanding Your Mate*. Grand Rapids, Michigan: Zondervan Publishing House, 1970.

Tournier, Paul. *To Understand Each Other*. Richmond, Virginia: John Knox Press, 1967.

SEX

LaHaye, Tim and Beverly. *The Act of Marriage: The Beauty of Sexual Love*. Grand Rapids, Michigan: The Zondervan Corporation, 1976.

Miles, Herbert. *Sexual Happiness in Marriage*. Grand Rapids, Michigan: Zondervan Publishing House, 1967.

Miles, Herbert. *Sexual Understanding Before Marriage*. Grand Rapids, Michigan: Zondervan Publishing House, 1971.

Rice, Shirley. *Physical Unity in Marriage*. The Tabernacle Church of Norfolk, 7120 Granby Street, Norfolk, Virginia, 1973.

Trobisch, Ingrid. *The Joy of Being a Woman*. New York: Harper & Row, Publishers, 1975.

Wheat, Ed and Gaye. *Intended for Pleasure*. Old Tappan, New Jersey: Fleming H. Revell Company, 1977

Wheat, Ed 'Sex Techniques and Sex Problems in Marriage," a series of tapes available from Bible Believers Cassettes, 130 North Spring, Springdale, Arkansas 72764.

DISCUSSION QUESTIONS FOR BETTER COMMUNICATION

THE following questions can be used to gain knowledge of each other whether as an engaged couple, as a newly married husband and wife, or even as "old married folk." In order for them to be most profitable, set apart some time for exploring feelings; then take a section which intrigues you and travel new roads of adventure, penetrating into unexplored territory of your minds and hearts. Use the questions to search, observe, analyze, and probe new vistas.

If you want to consider other questions in the same categories, consult Joseph B. Henry's *Fulfillment in Marriage* (Westwood, New Jersey: Fleming H. Revell Company, 1966), pages 56-79. The questions in this section are partly ours and partly adapted from Henry's book.

If there are difficult areas of communication in your marriage, begin with the easy topics . . . and use only the positive questions at first. Then progress to the topics you have problems discussing, and finally to those questions which may be painful but are imperative to explore. Begin with prayer . . . end with prayer. Let God be the third Person sitting in on these dialogues. And remember, with God all things *are* possible.

COMMUNICATION

1. On a scale from 1 to 100 (with 100 being high), how would you rate me as a communicator? What, in your opinion, would help me be a more effective communicator with you?

2. How free do you feel to share with me your fears, feelings, superstitions, opinions? What do I do that might make you afraid to share these with me?

3. What words, manners of speech, phrases, kinds of voices annoy you?

4. In what areas do you feel we may not be completely honest with each other, and how can we remedy this?

5. What, in your opinion, is the difference between argument and discussion? Am I more likely to argue or discuss with you? With other people?

6. How soon and in what way should we handle small problems that come up daily?

7. How do you feel when I make a suggestion for change? How can I better make these suggestions? (Or can I?)

8. Does it bother you when I ask, "What do you mean?" If so, why?

9. What do you think about reading books together and discussing the ideas presented?

10. When and on what subjects do you feel I can be stubborn and resisting to your point of view? How can we remedy this?

11. Do you feel generally that I am thinking with you or disagreeing?

12. Can you share ideas with me freely with the feeling that I will understand you? Do you think I face facts realistically?

13. Do you feel our silent communication is good? In other words, can you tell what I am thinking (by expression, nods, gestures, or just thought waves) in a group or just the two of us when we don't say anything? How could we improve on this "language without words"?

BACKGROUNDS AND BALANCE
1. In what areas do you feel that we are equals? Any that we are unequal?
2. How would you describe the role of a man? Of a woman?
3. How well do you feel your parents related to one another? What would you like to carry over from them? Avoid?
4. Is there any difference in our educational backgrounds that bothers you?
5. What could be some differences in our social backgrounds that might cause us conflict? Are there social habits, practices, and manners that I have that bother you? Are there some things that you feel are important that I am failing to do? (Seating you, meeting you at the door, etc.)
6. What are your ideas on integration? Would you let a child of ours marry one of another race?
7. What do you consider our areas of mutual interest? What would be interesting and fun to develop together?
8. How do you like men/women to dress? What are some suggestions you have about the way I dress?
9. Do you think economy or quality are more important?
10. What do you like to read? What areas do we have in common in reading? Do you like to read aloud together? Is this something we should work on?
11. What kind of humor do you enjoy?
12. What problem areas might we have in the way I spend money? The way you do? What would you economize on that I might not? Do you feel we can talk about these matters regularly without getting angry?

13. In your opinion, are our tastes similar or dissimilar? (In clothes, furniture, apartments, sports, reading, what we enjoy.) If not, in what areas and does it matter to us? What can we do about this? What about our taste in cars? Size of bed we should have? Pictures? Music? Books? Magazines?
14. Who should be responsible for the maintenance of the home? In what areas should there be division of responsibility? To whom?
15. What do you think about women working?
16. Who do you feel should manage the money in our home?
17. Do you like to operate on a budget?
18. What is your thinking on how much we should give from our income? What are your current areas of giving?
19. Do you like to have a savings plan? How important is it to you to save some money regularly?
20. What do you think about borrowing? From the family? From others?
21. Can we agree on a budget and each of us stick to it?

HEALTH

1. How much do you like to exercise? How much would you like for me to exercise? Is this important to you?
2. Do you have regular checkups by a doctor?
3. How much fresh air do you like at night?
4. Are you a slow riser? (Should I learn not to speak to you before breakfast?)
5. Is there anything in your family's medical history or in your own that I should be aware of?
6. How important is relaxation to you? How do you best relax? How can I help you in this?

ETHICS

1. Do you feel that most people are honest? Do you feel that it is really not honest to fudge a bit on income taxes, a child's age at a ticket window, about import duty?
2. Does it disturb you not to pay a bill on time? How important is it to you to have a good credit rating with everyone?
3. Do you regularly violate any traffic regulations? Which ones?
4. Do you feel I often exaggerate? Does this bother you?
5. How do you feel about keeping promises? About playing "tricks" on people?

CHILDREN

1. How many children do you want?
2. What are your thoughts on the discipline of children?
3. What do you feel about birth control and planning or spacing of children?
4. How soon do you want a child after marriage?
5. If we couldn't have children, how do you feel about adoption?
6. What changes would you make from your own childhood that relate to raising a family?
7. What are your ideas on working at being a good parent? (How can we best go about it? How important is it?)

FAMILY POLICIES

1. What differences have you noted in our backgrounds? Can we face these differences honestly and adjust to one another?

2. What are the family customs from your own up-bringing that you would like to continue in our family? How important is this to you?
3. Do you like to entertain? How much would you like it to be a part of your life? What sort of entertaining (casual, formal) do you prefer?
4. What are your thoughts on visiting parents and other relatives? On their visiting you?
5. What do you think about family anniversaries, birthdays, special occasions? What about gifts for these? How much would you spend on these gifts?
6. Do you feel you can be in close fellowship with your family and also be free to live your own life? Do you feel we have achieved this? In what areas do we need to work at this?
7. Do you think I do my share of work?
8. Do you feel we are in agreement about meal schedules, table practices, bedtimes, hours of sleep, house temperatures, how to spend weekends?
9. What do you think about a husband and wife having time away from their children? How often? What do you think about "dating"? How important in your priorities is this time with me?
10. Do you like animals? Do you feel animals should be kept outside?
11. If one of our parents were widowed or sick, what do you feel is our responsibility toward him/her?

RECREATION AND LEISURE
1. To you, what is the greatest way to spend a vacation? What is your second choice?
2. Do you like to travel? Camp out?
3. Do you like my friends? Who do you feel is a fun couple to spend a vacation with?

4. Do you like to go on vacations with just family or with other people?

5. What are your hobbies? How much time do you like to spend on them?

6. How much time do you feel should be spent watching TV? What are your favorite programs? What about going to movies? What rating?

7. What kinds of sports do you like? (Playing or watching)

8. What other kinds of things do you like? (Games, for example)

9. Do you always have to be busy or do you enjoy just "being lazy"?

HABITS

1. Do you think I am inclined to be overly neat or overly sloppy? What habits would you like for me to change? Do unwashed dishes, unmade beds, towels not hung well, papers not stacked neatly, pictures not hanging straight, and other similar things bother you? What specifically?

2. Do I have any personal idiosyncrasies or practices that annoy you? Do you think you can accept living with these if I cannot change? (The most often mentioned are: picking teeth, manner of chewing, spitting, sounds in eating, scratching, twitching, clearing the throat, snoring, sniffing, use of gum, use of tobacco, personal grooming, use of alcoholic beverages, use (or non-use) of colognes or perfumes, bathing and toilet practices, body odors, being chronically late, not hanging up clothes in the proper place, scattering apparel, not closing doors or drawers, offensive language, not replacing lids or caps, leaving the bathroom in a mess, mannerisms

of speech, perverted humor, off-beat ideas, over-meticulousness, messiness, lack of organization, prudishness, artificiality.)

SPIRITUAL THINGS

1. What is your concept of God? Christ? Sin? Man's relationship to God?
2. What are effective ways of coping with evil? Temptation?
3. How do you view death? Burial procedures?
4. What are your thoughts on the sources of real, deep inner peace of mind?
5. If I were enticed into sin, told you the truth about it and asked your forgiveness, what would be your response?
6. Where do you find your greatest security?
7. What to you are the ingredients of a truly wonderful way of living?

SEX

A. Questions to discuss before marriage:
1. Do you feel we are honest and open with each other in talking about sex?
2. Do you feel we have the same standards?
3. What do you feel is the purpose of sex?

B. Questions to discuss after marriage:
1. What causes you special pleasure?
2. Do you wish I would initiate sex more often? Less often?
3. How do you feel a woman's moods relate to her menstrual cycle?

UNDERSTANDING

1. What do you feel are my strengths? My weaknesses?

2. How do you think I can best help you when you are depressed?

3. How can I best encourage you? What are ways I am an encouragement to you now? What ways that I might be?

4. In what areas do you feel I don't understand you?

5. Do you feel you have a real understanding of men? Of women? Do I?

6. How do you see yourself as far as temperament type is concerned? How do you see me?

7. Do you think personalities *can* be changed? *Should* be changed?

8. What is your response to a woman crying? To a man crying? To an outburst of temper? What would you like my response to be to these?

9. Who is the most understanding person you have ever known? What about that person makes you say that?

10. Do you feel that I am quick to mention a fault or flaw in you? When I do, do you feel I mean to help? What is your reaction to my suggestions? How could I suggest better?

11. Do you think I sympathize with you at a deep level? With others?

12. What are some ways I can demonstrate that I love you that I am not now doing?

13. What are two of the happiest things that ever happened to you? What brings you the most happiness today?

14. What has been the hardest experience of your life? The saddest? What are the things that cause you the most anxiety today?